FINGERFOOD

FINGERFOOD

bite-size food for cocktail parties

Elsa Petersen-Schepelern

photography by William Lingwood

RYLAND
PETERS
& SMALL

LONDON NEW YORK

First published in USA in 1999
This edition published in 2005
by Ryland Peters & Small, Inc.
519 Broadway, 5th Floor, New York, NY 10012
www.rylandpeters.com

10 9 8 7 6 5 4 3

Library of Congress Cataloging-in-Publication Data
Petersen-Schepelern, Elsa.
    Finger food / Elsa Petersen-Schepelern ;
    photography by William Lingwood.
        p. cm.
    Originally published: Alexandria, Va. : Time-Life
Books, c1999
    Includes index.
    ISBN 1-84172-363-0
    1. Appetizers. I. Title.

TX740 .P464 2002
641.8'12--dc21   2002024848

ISBN-10: 1 84172 990 6
ISBN-13: 978 1 84172 990 9

Notes
Spoon measurements are level.

Uncooked or partially cooked eggs should not
be served to the very old or frail, the very young,
pregnant women, or those with compromised
immune systems.
ⓥ Indicates recipes suitable for vegetarians.

Designer Sonya Nathoo
Editor Maddalena Bastianelli
Production Patricia Harrington
Art Director Gabriella Le Grazie
Publishing Director Alison Starling

Food Stylists Sunil Vijayakar, Maddalena
Bastianelli, Elsa Petersen-Schepelern
Prop Stylist Mary Norden

Printed in China

contents

fingerfood

Serve a mixture of prepare-ahead and last-minute assemblies—recipes ranging from spiced nuts or salmon brochettes, to mini pita pockets. Above all, choose recipes that will help to take the panic out of partying!

What kind of party?

The recipes in this book are designed to be served as fingerfood at a cocktail party. Usually such parties last for 2–3 hours. If you've asked people for a longer time, then you should also serve them several more substantial dishes.

You can also use the recipes as nibbles to serve with cocktails before dinner—just choose your dishes well, so you don't fill people up before the meal. Take care with quantities too—many's the time I've had to wrest the Flat Beans with Hummus from people who've come to dinner, in case they didn't have any room left for the main event.

How many people?

The size of your party will depend on the size of your house—or garden—and the capacity of your kitchen. In a small apartment, 6 people might be the limit. In a larger house or a garden, the numbers might swell to dozens, or even hundreds (though if you've invited hundreds, call in the professionals!)

Recipe choice

Choose 4–6 items per hour—several easy things from the first chapter, then one each from other chapters.

Sweet things, like ice cream and cake should be served towards the end of the party—they signal "finale."

Unless you have a large house, where cooking smells won't invade the party, cook fried items the morning or day before, then reheat in the oven.

Recipe order

Serve treats like oysters, shrimp, or caviar first, with fanfare.

In fact, treat your party menu like an ordinary meal. Serve light and fresh things first, such as soups or morsels wrapped in leaves, then more substantial foods like sushi or bruschetta—to help soak up the alcohol. Follow these with rice, bread, or tarts, then the more substantial dishes of meat or poultry.

Then something light and salady, then savory and cheesy, then sweet. Most people can't drink any more alcohol after sweet things.

One thing at a time

Serve just one kind of food at a time. Remember those who don't eat meat, or can't eat the kind you're offering. So include a vegetarian or chicken option. Vegetarian recipes in this book are marked Ⓥ beside the serving quantity.

Waiters and sous chefs

Depending on the size of your party, it's only sensible to have helpers—family or friends, professional waiters, or chefs.

Hire them far in advance, and brief them well before they start serving. They must know what to do, how you want them to do it, and what they're serving.

FOOD FACTS

How much food?

It depends how long your party will be, and how many cooks will be available to prepare the food.

I think that one cook—that's you—can cope with about 8 different dishes, but only if you are able to prepare at least half of them in advance (that means recipes such as Anchovy Pinwheels, Cheese Straws, or Mini Christmas Cakes).

Prepare each dish on the assembly-line principle, completing one task before beginning the next.

Serve 4–6 items each hour per guest, so for 30 people for 2 hours you need 8–12 different dishes—that's at least 240 items, so plan ahead.

What kind of food?

The best collections of fingerfoods include a range of textures and flavors and several different preparation and cooking methods to make life easier for the cook. Include:

• Crunchy things, like fries, chips, or wontons.

• Savory, salty things like Anchovy Pinwheels and nuts.

• Substantial things to soak up the alcohol (pizza and bruschetta).

• Creamy things like Leaves with Hummus and Tabbouleh Salad, or Blini with Cream Cheese and Smoked Salmon.

• Sweet Things (optional) as a final treat, particularly if it's a special occasion like Christmas or a birthday.

Special dietary requirements

Remember some of your guests may have special requirements. Mostly, they will organize for themselves which of your dishes they would like to or can eat. But think of them when you're planning your menu.

• If they're dieters, have pity on them. Don't make every single thing either fried or creamy, or packed with carbohydrates.

• If some have religious taboos, don't serve too many dishes made with pork, seafood, or beef—or avoid them altogether.

• Some may be vegetarian, so make sure there are several things they can eat (and make sure your waiters know which they are). Vegetarian dishes in this book have been marked with a special symbol ⓥ after the serving quantity.

• If some guests are vegan (no animal products of any kind, including eggs, cheese, or cream), point them toward vegetable sushi or Flat Beans and Hummus, and have some bruschetta that will suit them.

• Some people have allergies, for instance to peanuts, gluten, chiles, or shrimp. Most allergic people are alert for foods that may cause problems, but if you know your friends have allergies like these, either leave out that ingredient or make sure your waiters know which foods contain the problem element.

Drips
Fingerfood should be confined to things that can be eaten in one bite—or two at most. Above all, it must not be unwieldy—the kind of food that tumbles or drips down people's shirt fronts.

Your guests should be able to hold a drink in one hand and the food in the other. Or perhaps both items in one hand, leaving the other free for talking.

Forward preparation
If you're making many different bite-size foods, plan ahead. Prepare some dishes in advance, freezing some, chilling others, and storing yet others in airtight containers for 1–2 days.

Preheat your oven for about 15 minutes before the party starts so you can reheat some ready-prepared dishes and give a quick final cooking to others. I set mine at 400°F throughout the party. I also have a collection of electronic timers which beep madly as each item is ready. Then you won't miscalculate and burn the food.

Food safety

When you have a party, you're catering for large numbers of people and storing larger quantities of food than usual.

Remember to keep food preparation areas, utensils, and hands scrupulously clean. Before and after cooking, heat and cool foods quickly, so they spend as little time as possible in the danger zone for microbe-multiplication. Do not put hot or warm food in the refrigerator, which should remain at 32–40°F.

Dry or salty items, such as nuts, chips, caperberries, or olives, are safe, because microbes don't flourish under such conditions.

When you reheat, do so thoroughly (without burning the food to a crisp). It should be kept at 145°F or hotter until ready to serve. However, when you serve the food, don't serve it blisteringly hot, or people will burn themselves.

How much food can you fit in your own refrigerator and freezer? When you're catering for lots of people, you won't necessarily have room for it all. That means you must borrow other people's refrigerators and freezers—or even hire them.

PARTY DRINKS

How much?

Better too much than too little. Be generous! Most suppliers will let you return what you don't use. Some people will drink—others won't—and you may not know until they get there. Remember to have enough for both.

Champagne

My favorite party drink is champagne. For a 2-hour party, allow about $\frac{1}{2}$ bottle per guest, for a 3-hour party, $\frac{3}{4}$ bottle for each person. That looks after the people who drink more and those who drink nothing at all.

There are 6 glasses in a bottle—or 8 if you're mixing it to make Kir (page 132) or a Champagne Cocktail (page 139).

Serve a light, dry kind—such as Mumm, Cuvée Napa, a cava, or Green Point—it doesn't have to be French.

Wine

Again, about ½ bottle per person. When serving wine at a party, you'll probably find people prefer white, with a few die-hards who don't drink anything but red. Make sure it's good quality and not so distinctive that people's palates will pall after 2 hours of it.

The ratio of white to red will be different in summer and winter. In summer, allow 3 bottles of white to 1 of red, and in winter, make them equal—but you know your own guests. But let's face it, if you allow 1 bottle per person, you can always serve the leftovers at your next dinner party.

Cocktails

Cocktails are a stylish choice, but limit yourself to 2–3 kinds—one each from the gin-vodka family, the brandy-whisky group, and the hold-onto-your-hat gang, such as tequila and rum.

If you don't have bar staff, and since it's difficult to prepare cocktails in advance, choose something easy to make. Cocktails can be pretty intoxicating, so many people like to have just one or two, then move onto something else.

Garnishes

Order lots of limes and lemons, cut them into slices and wedges in advance, and cover with plastic wrap. Other garnishes will depend on the drinks you're serving—olives and lemon zest for Martinis, maraschino cherries for Manhattans, cucumber for Pimm's, and mint for juleps and mohitos.

Liquor

If a person is a whiskey drinker, he (and he's often a he) won't be fobbed off with wine. There are 16 measures in a 750 ml bottle of whiskey and other spirits. Three is all most people will manage in a 2-hour party.

It's not necessary to offer every kind spirit. The three most popular—bourbon, vodka, and gin—are probably enough, though tequila and whiskey also have their followers.

Mixers

Mixers should include sparkling and still water, soda, cola, tonic, gingerale, orange, grapefruit, and tomato juice.

Punch-bowl drinks

Good for a big party, these drinks can be prepared or part-prepared in advance. Try Planter's Punch, Sangria, non-alcoholic punch, Glögg, and so on.

The very strong ones, like Planter's Punch, contain about the same amount of alcohol as a strong measure of spirits, so cater accordingly.

The lighter, wine-based drinks such as Sangria contain only a little less alcohol than wine itself, so cater as for wine.

Bottled water and soft drinks

Allow 1 bottle for every 3–4 people, and divide the quantity between still and sparkling water.

Designated Drivers and other teetotalists will be delighted if you make an effort with their drinks, and even the drinkers will be glad of something fresh when they decide to stop drinking.

And remember—lots of ice!

spoons, cups, and quickies

Who said party food had to be difficult and complicated? This chapter shows that simple but delicious ingredients, simply served, can taste wonderful and look spectacular. And they make life easier for the cook.

smoked salmon brochettes

This is exactly the kind of party food that is neither difficult or complicated. It's a simple idea that can be prepared in the morning, covered with plastic wrap and refrigerated until just before serving (it will taste better if you let it come back to room temperature first).

8 oz. smoked salmon
(about 10 slices)

finely grated zest of 2 lemons

freshly cracked black pepper

Makes about 30

Cut slices of smoked salmon lengthwise into long strips, about ½ inch wide and 4 inches long. (Most slices give about 3 strips.) Carefully thread the strips onto toothpicks.

Arrange the loaded sticks on a serving platter and sprinkle with finely grated lemon zest and cracked black pepper.

ice-cold prairie oysters

The Prairie Oyster is a time-honored hangover cure—a raw egg yolk, Tabasco, salt, and pepper. I've always thought that adding tomato juice and hair of the dog in vodka form could only be an improvement. I've replaced the egg yolk with a real oyster, and the result is utterly delicious! Serve this as a one-off canapé-cum-cocktail when people first arrive. Make sure all the ingredients are ice-cold, and keep the vodka in the freezer.

3 cups tomato juice
2 cups ice-cold vodka
juice of 6 limes or 2 large lemons
a dash of Tabasco, or to taste
crushed ice
12 freshly shucked oysters
sea salt and freshly ground black pepper

To serve (optional)

sprigs of fresh mint or a curl of lime zest
mini wedges or slivers of lime

Serves 12

Put the tomato juice, vodka, lime or lemon juice, and Tabasco in a pitcher half-full of crushed ice. Stir well. (To make in advance, omit the ice and chill well. Add the ice prior to serving.)

Put 1 oyster in each of 12 shot glasses, aquavit, or sherry glasses, add the chilled vodka mixture, then top with a mint leaf or lime zest, a little salt and pepper, and a lime wedge speared with a toothpick.

For people who don't like oysters, omit the oysters and serve the tomato mixture as a Bloody Mary.

Variation Before you start, rub a lemon wedge around the rim of each glass, and press the rim into a saucer of salt, as if you were making a Margarita.

spoonfuls of caviar

A spoonful of caviar is incredibly luxurious and a rare treat for most of us. Serve it early in the party, perhaps first-off, with a shot glass of ice-cold vodka. Champagne or white wine is also a good choice!

Unless you're very rich, confine this spectacular dish to small gatherings! One small 2 oz. can of caviar will serve 8 people. Beluga is sold in a blue can, followed by Oscietre in yellow, and Sevruga in red. Though Beluga is the most highly regarded, the slightly less expensive Sevruga is fine for a party.

Remember—never serve caviar in a metal spoon. Use bone, wood, glass—even plastic.

2 oz. canned caviar or salmon keta

Serves about 8

Using a plastic teaspoon, carefully take one spoonful out of the can, without breaking any of the eggs.

Put into a serving teaspoon, smoothing it carefully (remember—no metal!). Repeat until you have enough for each guest. Arrange the spoons on a plate (rectangular is better) and serve.

Variation Other kinds of caviar are also delicious. Try Salmon Keta, Trout Eggs, Tuna Eggs, Lumpfish, Mullet, Sea Urchin, or American Caviar.

For larger gatherings, other dishes can be served on spoons—or try them in leaves (pages 78–81).

spoonfuls of goat cheese Ⓥ

Put 1 cup goat cheese, ½ cup cream, 1 cup snipped chives, salt and pepper in a bowl and mix well.

Using a melon baller or the smallest ice cream scoop dipped into boiling water, scoop out balls of the mixture and set them in teaspoons or Chinese porcelain soup spoons. Arrange the spoons on a platter and serve.

spoonfuls of spicy thai salad

Mix 2 cups cooked crabmeat in a bowl with 2 teaspoons lime juice, 2 teaspoons fish sauce or soy sauce, 1 teaspoon sugar and 2 chopped red chiles. Serve as above.

Use mini waxpaper cups or demitasse coffee cups to serve **hot soups**, or shot glasses for cold ones.

sweet potato soup

1 onion, finely chopped

2 garlic cloves, crushed

1 inch fresh ginger, grated

2 stalks lemongrass, finely chopped

1 tablespoon red Thai curry paste

1 tablespoon lime juice

3 tablespoons peanut oil

1 lb. sweet potatoes (about 2 large)

2 cups canned coconut milk

2 cups chicken or vegetable stock

sea salt and freshly ground black pepper

To serve

finely grated kaffir lime zest

finely sliced red chiles

Serves 24 ⓥ

Put the onion, garlic, ginger, lemongrass, chiles or curry paste, lime juice, and 2 tablespoons of the peanut oil in a blender or spice grinder (coffee mill) and blend until smooth.

Heat a wok, then swirl in the remaining oil. Add the spice paste and cook gently for 5 minutes. Do not let it burn.

Add the sweet potatoes, coconut milk, and stock. Simmer, uncovered, until the sweet potatoes are soft. Transfer to the blender and pulse until smooth. Season to taste, reheat if necessary, and serve in small containers. Top with grated lime zest and sliced red chile.

pea soup with mint

Frozen peas are fine for this soup. For the harassed party host, I give a microwave-blender version.

1 tablespoon olive oil

8 slices pancetta (as thin as possible)

3½ cups frozen peas

4 cups boiling chicken stock

sea salt and freshly ground black pepper

mint tips, to serve

Serves 24

Heat the olive oil in a skillet, add the pancetta, and sauté until crisp. Remove and drain on paper towels.

Microwave the peas on HIGH according to the package instructions. Transfer to a blender, add 1 cup stock, salt, and pepper. Blend to a purée, then add the remaining stock and blend again. Taste and adjust the seasoning, then add extra stock or boiling water if too thick.

Pour into waxpaper cups, demitasse coffee cups, or heatproof glasses. Serve topped with crisp pancetta and a mint tip.

Note The soup will thicken as it cools, so make it a little thinner than you want the end result to be.

"Quickies" are invaluable as fingerfood, because one or more of them can be prepared earlier, covered to keep them moist, then brought out between your more time-consuming efforts.

oysters on ice

There is nothing better than a plate of super-fresh chilled oysters still in their liquid.

Arrange them on a plate of sea salt and seaweed, prepare them properly without any specks of shell, and with the oyster properly detached from the shell. Add lemon wedges if you like (though I think oysters are better absolutely plain).

Serve with chilled champagne or white wine, but never ever with whiskey!

These **quick assemblies** are so simple that they don't need much in the way of a recipe, just a few serving ideas.

grilled indian cheese

Other cheeses, such as Italian provolone or farmer's cheese, can be used for this dish, but the original uses Indian paneer.

peanut or mustard oil or ghee (clarified butter), for brushing

1 lb. paneer, provolone, or farmer's cheese, cut into ¾-inch cubes

Makes about 8 ⓥ

Brush a stove-top grill-pan or skillet with oil or ghee. Briefly grill or sauté the cubes of cheese until lightly browned on all sides. Serve warm or cool.

Note Paneer is sold in Asian stores. To make it yourself, put 4 cups whole milk in a saucepan, bring to a boil, then stir in 2 tablespoons fresh lemon juice and 2 tablespoons plain yogurt. When the milk curdles, pour into a strainer lined with cheesecloth and let drain for 3 hours. Cover with cheesecloth, put a plate on top and a heavy food can on top of that. Chill for 4 hours or overnight until the cheese hardens a little (the longer you leave it, the harder it will be), then invert and cut into cubes. Drain on a clean cloth, then use.

flat beans and hummus

This dish is so simple—and incredibly popular. I have served it with drinks before dinner parties and people have loved it so much they've almost had no room for the rest of the food!

1 lb. flat beans or runner beans

1 cup hummus, either store-bought or homemade

To serve (optional)

2 teaspoons extra-virgin olive oil

freshly cracked black pepper

Serves 6–8 Ⓥ

Top and tail the beans, then cut them diagonally into 1–2-inch sections.

Spoon the hummus into a small bowl and swirl the top. Sprinkle with olive oil and pepper, if using.

Put the bowl on a serving platter with the beans beside.

plunged shrimp
with chilli mojo

An easy recipe with one simple requirement—perfect
shrimp. Test before you buy: texture is everything—they
must be firm, with tightly curled tails.

1–3 tail-on cooked or uncooked shrimp per person,
depending on size

Chilli Mojo (page 41)

Serves 1

If using uncooked shrimp, insert a toothpick at the neck
of each shrimp and pull out the dark vein.

Bring a large saucepan of well-salted water to a boil (you can
also add a sheet of kombu seaweed, removing it just before
boiling point). Plunge in the shrimp and cook just until the
flesh is opaque (about 3 minutes, depending on the size
of the shrimp).

Remove with a wire basket or slotted spoon and plunge
them immediately into a large bowl of ice water to stop the
cooking (don't leave them there too long, or you'll wash
away the flavor). Remove and chill over ice.

Remove the shells and legs, but leave the tail fins intact
(keep the shells in the freezer and use to make bisques or
other seafood soups).

Put the shrimp on a plate or tray with a bowl of Chile Mojo
and serve.

Shrimp make superb fingerfood. Buy them with the tail fin intact to use as a handle.

plantain chips

Plantain is the cooking banana just packed with fiber (if you can't find plantains, use green bananas). Cook as many chips as possible, because they're eaten almost as fast as you can make them.

6 plantains, green if possible, or yellow, but not black, or 12 green bananas

peanut or safflower oil, for frying

To serve, your choice of

mild chile powder

chile sauce

Serves about 20 ⓥ

• Make other Caribbean chips with other vegetables such as 1 lb. sweet potatoes, 1 lb. yams, such as eddoes, yellow coco, or Ghana yam, 1 lb. pumpkin, deseeded but unpeeled, or 1 lb. parsnips.

To peel the plantains, cut off the points at either end, then run the tip of your knife down the length of the fruit, just piercing the skin. Do this in 3–4 places. Carefully run your thumbs under the skin, easing it off. (Another way is to soak the slit plantains in warm water for 10 minutes before peeling.)

Using a vegetable peeler or mandoline, cut long lengthwise strips off the plantain. To make thicker chips, as shown, cut diagonally with a knife.

Meanwhile, fill a wok one-third full of oil and heat to 375°F. (I prefer a wok because you're not wasting lots of extra oil in the corners.) Alternatively, fill a deep-fryer with oil and heat to the recommended temperature.

Add the plantain strips in batches and fry until crisp and golden. Remove with a slotted spoon and drain on paper towels.

When all the chips are cooked, serve immediately, or let cool and transfer to an airtight container until ready to use.

To serve, sprinkle sparingly with chile powder (don't make it too hot—some people won't like it) and serve in twists or cones of paper.

oven-dried tomatoes

I think sun-dried tomatoes are rather leathery in texture and overwhelming in flavor, except when used to make pesto. However, if you oven-dry fresh tomatoes until they've collapsed, they are wonderful as toppings for bruschetta and pizza. If you keep roasting them until they're half-dry, they make a delicious if less crunchy addition to the chip repertoire.

12 small tomatoes (the next size up from cherries or grapes) or mini plum tomatoes

sugar

sea salt

2–3 garlic cloves, cut into fine slivers (optional)

Makes 24 ⓥ

Cut the tomatoes in half crosswise and cut out the dense core with a small, sharp knife. Arrange apart on baking trays. Top each half with a pinch of sugar and a few flakes of sea salt. Push 2 fine slivers of garlic, if using, into the seed section of each tomato half.

Roast in a preheated oven at 400°F for about 1 hour. Test after 30 minutes and 45 minutes. When collapsed and browned but still soft, they can be used as a topping for pizza and bruschetta, or served as a vegetable.

Cook for about 15 minutes longer and they will have dried out enough to be served as a nibble, as shown.

fish and chips

Assemble all the ingredients for the tempura batter, but do not mix it.

Fill a wok one-third full of oil and heat to 375°F. Alternatively, fill a deep-fryer with oil and heat to the recommended temperature.

Add the potato strips in batches and fry for about 2 minutes until creamy-gold. Remove with a slotted spoon and spread out to drain on paper towels. When all the strips have been fried, reheat the oil and fry them again until crisp and golden. Drain on paper towels and keep them warm in the oven. They should be so crisp they rustle together.

Skim the oil and reheat to 375°F.

Put a large bowl to the left of the wok (if you're right-handed) and a serving platter lined with paper towels to the right. Have the fish to the left of the bowl. Put the batter ingredients in the bowl and mix quickly with chopsticks, leaving as lumpy as possible, and with a rim of flour left unmixed around the bowl.

Using long chopsticks or tongs, dip each piece of fish quickly in the batter, then gently in the hot oil. Fry until golden, remove, and drain on paper towels.

To serve, put a pinch of the fries in each container and add a piece of tempura fish. Line them up vertically, so people don't drop any on the floor.

Serve immediately. If you need to reheat them a little, put the paper cones in the oven with the door open for a few minutes.

6 large potatoes, cut into matchsticks

1 lb. salmon fillet, sliced in half lengthwise, then crosswise into ⅓-inch wide strips

safflower or peanut oil, for frying

sea salt

Tempura batter

5 tablespoons cornstarch

5 tablespoons all-purpose flour

1 teaspoon baking powder

5 teaspoons safflower or peanut oil

¾ cup club soda or beer

Serves 20

Yes, I know you can buy **toasted nuts**, but it's easy to toast your own, and you can add all sorts of delicious spices to them to make them more personal.

spiced toasted nuts

Your choice of freshly ground or crushed spices, such as

cinnamon sticks

cardamom

nutmeg

mild chile flakes

sesame seeds

cumin seeds

paprika

ginger

black pepper

grated citrus zest

Thai 7-spice

Japanese 7-spice

Your choice of fresh, raw nuts, about 1 oz. or 2 tablespoons per person, such as

peanuts

cashews

macadamias

almonds

pecans

1 tablespoon sunflower oil, for roasting (optional)

sea salt flakes

Serves 8 ⓥ

These nuts look wonderful served in tiny individual cones, dishes, or boxes. People can hold a drink and a cone in one hand and pick out the nuts with the other. It avoids all those anxieties about many hands dipping into the bowl of nuts. The number one rule is—fresh nuts and freshly ground spices.

Break up the cinnamon sticks and grind them to a powder with a spice grinder or mortar and pestle.

Wipe out the mill, then grind the black seeds from the green cardamom pods (or buy them already podded—if you do it yourself, the seeds can be a little sticky). If using nutmeg, grate whole ones with a nutmeg grater, or on the finest side of a box grater.

To roast the nuts, heat a dry skillet, add one kind of nut and cook, shaking the pan, until they're aromatic and slightly golden. You must stay with them and keep shaking, or the nuts will burn and be spoiled.

When ready, tip them into a wide, shallow bowl, then sprinkle with salt and one of the spices or citrus zest.

If preferred, you can cook the nuts with 1 tablespoon sunflower oil, but your guests will love the flavor of dry-toasted nuts and thank you for saving them from that tiny extra drop of oil.

To serve, put about 2 tablespoons of the nuts into each paper twist, tiny china bowl, or folded mini box, arrange in a basket, and serve.

Like many of the ideas in this book, **dips** are mix-and-match with other recipes

Mexican Salsa is good as a dipping sauce, on bruschetta, or mixed with chicken and served in baby lettuce leaves.

1 large red chile, halved

1 mango, seeded and chopped

½ papaya, seeded and chopped

1 small red onion, finely diced

juice of 2 limes

juice of 1 orange

2 garlic cloves, minced

2 teaspoons sugar

a pinch of sea salt

Makes about 2 ¾ cups ⓥ

Broil the chile until the skin blisters (not too long, or the flesh will become bitter). Remove, then scrape off and discard the burnt skin and all the membranes. Chop the flesh.

Put all the ingredients in a bowl and stir. Mash a little with a fork if necessary.

Eggplant purée or **Baba Ganoush** is one of the greatest dishes from the Middle East.

1 large eggplant

2 fat garlic cloves, minced

½ cup tahini paste

½ cup lemon juice

sea salt

1 small bunch parsley, finely chopped

Makes about 2¾ cups ⓥ

Prick the eggplant all over with a fork. Cook in a preheated oven at about 400°F for about 30 minutes, or until the outside is charred and the inside is soft and fluffy. (Some traditional recipes suggest that the eggplant be charred over an open flame, or under a broiler, but I was taught by a splendid Polish cook, who just put it in the oven.)

Peel off and discard the charred skin, rinsing off any remaining black bits with water. Put the peeled flesh in a food processor with the garlic, tahini, lemon juice, and salt. Pulse to a purée, add salt to taste, then transfer to a serving bowl. Sprinkle with parsley and serve warm or at room temperature.

Rouille, the Mediterranean mayonnaise-style sauce, is perfect with seafood. **Aioli** is made in the same way, omitting the chiles and bread from the recipe below.

3 garlic cloves, minced

2 large dried chiles, soaked for 15 minutes in hot water, then seeded and finely chopped

1 slice bread, dipped in water, squeezed dry

sea salt

2 egg yolks

1 egg

about ⅓–½ cup olive oil

Makes about 1 cup ⓥ

Put the garlic, chiles, bread, salt, egg yolks, and egg in a blender or small food processor and work to a paste. Add the oil, drop by drop at first, then more quickly, making a thick, creamy sauce.

Mexican **Chile Mojos** are a little more liquid than salsas.

¼ cup chopped fresh flat-leaf parsley

1 tablespoon chopped oregano or marjoram

a pinch of sea salt

a pinch of sugar

3 garlic cloves, minced

grated zest of 1 lime

½ cup freshly squeezed lime juice

1 large red chile, cored, seeded, and finely chopped, plus 1 small red chile, sliced (optional)

Makes about 1 cup ⓥ

Put the herbs, salt, sugar, garlic, lime zest, and lime juice in a blender and work until smooth. Taste and add more sugar if necessary. Transfer to a serving dish and stir in the chopped chile.

spanish potato tortilla

This omelet is one of the simplest and most satisfying Spanish tapas. To serve more people, make several separate tortillas, don't just increase the quantity of ingredients.

1½ lb. potatoes
1½ cups olive oil
1 onion, thinly sliced
sea salt
6 eggs
2 red bell peppers, peeled, cored, seeded, and chopped (optional)

Makes 12 ⓥ

Peel and rinse the potatoes, then cut into ½-inch cubes and pat dry.

Heat the oil in a deep, heavy skillet, then add the potatoes and cook for 20–30 minutes, stirring from time to time, until softened but not browned.

Remove from the skillet and drain in a colander. Sprinkle with salt. Pour all except 2 tablespoons of the oil into a bowl. Add the onion to the skillet and sauté gently until softened but not browned. Transfer to the colander with a slotted spoon.

Beat the eggs lightly with a fork. Gently mix in the potatoes and peppers, if using.

Pour off the cooking oil, then heat a film of fresh oil in the base of the skillet, add the potato and egg mixture, and shake the pan a couple of times. Cook for 2 minutes or until set.

Cover the skillet with a flat lid or plate, then, holding the lid with one hand and the pan with the other, quickly upturn it, then slide the omelet back into the pan. Cook the other side for about 1–2 minutes. Transfer to a large plate and let cool. When cool, cut into 1-inch squares. Serve with toothpicks.

grilled asparagus

Grilling produces a delicious flavor, but you can also microwave or steam the asparagus, plunge into cold water, then drain and plunge into ice water. Drain and serve. Freshly grated Parmesan cheese, plain sea salt flakes, Aioli (page 41), or chile oil mixed with rice vinegar are all perfect accompaniments.

1–3 asparagus spears per person
olive oil, for brushing
sea salt, for sprinkling
Serves 1 ⓥ

Brush a stove-top grill-pan with olive oil, add the asparagus and press them down with a spatula. Cook for 2 minutes on each side (they should be barely cooked), then arrange, tips all one way, on a serving plate.

Alternatively, cook in a microwave for about 2 minutes or in a steamer. Test for doneness (they should be quite firm and crisp), steam or microwave a little longer if necessary, then either serve immediately or drain and plunge into ice water to stop the cooking. Drain again, then arrange as before.

When cooled, they can be kept, covered with plastic wrap, for 1–2 hours before serving.

toasts, buns, pizza, and tarts

Savory toppings and fillings for toasts, buns, pizza, and tarts can be used interchangeably with many of the recipes in this chapter, and with others in the book.

crisp toasts and grilled bruschetta

Easy, mini versions of everyone's favorite sandwich bases. Try toppings such as Onion Marmalade (right), Parma ham, Parmesan shavings, halved cherry tomatoes, caperberries, anchovies, or choose from the list on page 58.

1 baguette or 4 small ciabatta loaves, cut into ½-inch slices

Makes about 30 ⓥ

To make Crisp Toasts, arrange the baguette slices apart on a baking tray and cook in a preheated oven at 400°F until lightly biscuit-colored. Take care—don't let them become too crisp or they will break when touched.

Remove from the oven and cool on a wire rack. They can be kept in an airtight container for up to 1 week. When ready to serve, crisp them again in the oven for a few minutes.

To make **Grilled Bruschetta**, put the sliced ciabatta or baguette on a stove-top grill-pan or outdoor grill and cook until toasted and lined.

onion marmalade

Delicious caramelized onions can be used in lots of ways—on pizzas, in tarts, on hot dogs and hamburgers, or in leaf scoops.

2 lb. onions, preferably red, finely sliced

½ cup olive oil

1 bay leaf

1 tablespoon sugar

a pinch of sea salt

1 tablespoon red wine vinegar

1 tablespoon crème de cassis

¼ teaspoon ground allspice (optional)

Makes 2 cups ⓥ

Put the onions, oil, bay leaf, sugar, and salt in a wide skillet over moderate heat for about 2 minutes. Reduce the heat, cover, and simmer for about 15 minutes until the onions begin to soften. Stir every few minutes.

Add the vinegar, crème de cassis, and allspice, if using. Cook, stirring occasionally, until the onions have become translucent and caramelized, about 15–30 minutes more. Turn gently with tongs from time to time. Remove, cool, and transfer to a lidded container until ready to use. The marmalade will keep in the refrigerator for 1–2 days.

danish smørrebrød
(open sandwiches)

1 square loaf light rye bread (crusts removed if you like), sliced

lightly salted butter, for spreading

Toppings such as

pâté, beets (opposite), and parsley

tiny shrimp, lemon zest, and dill

smoked or poached salmon, sour cream, and chopped dill

pickled herring, baby lettuce, and crumbled hard-cooked egg

smoked ham, blue cheese, and chives

Makes about 48

I include these because I'm Danish, and because the Danes thought of these long before anyone decided bruschetta was the best thing to do with sliced bread. The only thing to remember is you need great bread, good-quality butter, and the freshest toppings. Traditionally, smørrebrød are made with halved, rectangular slices of rye bread—but if you cut them in half again, the little squares will make more manageable fingerfood.

Spread the bread lightly with butter. Cut each slice of bread in half to make rectangles and in half again to form squares. Pile toppings of your choice on the bread and serve as soon as possible. (The butter will prevent the toppings from making the bread soggy for a while, but don't wait around!)

spiced beets

The perfect accompaniment for pâté—and good with other party food in this book. Sterilize the jars by washing in a dishwasher and filling while still hot.

2 lb. small cooked beets (boiled)

1 tablespoon whole cloves

3 cinnamon sticks, broken

1¼ cups white wine vinegar

⅔ cup sugar

Makes about 3 jars, 1 pint each ⓥ

Cut off the tops and bottoms of the beets and slip off the skins.

Slice the beets thinly and arrange the slices in sterilized preserving jars. Tuck the cloves and cinnamon sticks down the sides.

Put the vinegar, ⅔ cup water, and sugar in a small saucepan, bring to a boil, and simmer until the sugar has dissolved. Pour into the jars until the beets are completely covered (make extra vinegar mixture if necessary—the quantity will depend on the size of your jars). Seal the jars immediately and use within 7 days.

mini chile corn muffins

1⅓ cups yellow cornmeal

1⅓ cups all-purpose flour

1 tablespoon baking powder

a pinch of sea salt

2 large eggs, lightly beaten

1¼ cups milk

3 tablespoons melted butter, plus extra for greasing

2 large fresh red chiles, deseeded and finely chopped

3 scallions, white and green, finely sliced

Pancetta, Avocado, and Cilantro

1 tablespoon olive oil

12 thin slices pancetta, prosciutto, or finely sliced bacon, cut crosswise into 1½-inch pieces

2 large ripe Hass avocados

lemon juice, for brushing

cilantro leaves

two deep 12-hole mini muffin pans, greased

Makes about 42

To prepare the muffins in advance:
- *Store in an airtight container for up to 2 days.*
- *Bag, label, and freeze for up to 1 month.*
- *Defrost for 20 minutes at room temperature.*
- *Reheat in the oven at 400°F for about 5 minutes before splitting and filling.*

If you're not a chile fan, leave them out of this mixture—and you can of course use your favorite fillings instead of the one used here.

Put the cornmeal, flour, baking powder, and salt in a large bowl and mix well. Mix in the eggs, milk, butter, chopped chiles, and scallions.

Using a teaspoon, spoon the batter into the prepared muffin pans to about two-thirds full. Bake in a preheated oven at 400°F for about 15 minutes until firm and lightly golden. Remove from the oven and transfer to a wire rack to cool.

Grease the muffin pans again, add mixture as before, bake and cool as before. Repeat until all the muffin mixture has been used. Eat warm on the day of baking or store and reheat as listed left.

To prepare the filling, heat the oil in a skillet, add the pieces of pancetta and sauté until crisp. Drain on paper towels.

When ready to serve, split the tops off the muffins, cut the avocado into ½-inch thick slices, then into muffin-sized wedges. If the avocado is very ripe, scoop out the flesh with a teaspoon instead. Put 1 piece of avocado in each muffin, top with a slice of crisp pancetta and a cilantro leaf. Put the tops back on the muffins and serve. If the lids are a bit unstable, spear the whole thing together with a toothpick.

cocktail blini

Blini are the one Russian dish that has migrated around the world to smart restaurants and parties everywhere. They could have been specially designed as fingerfood in fact.

1 cup buckwheat flour or half-and-half with all-purpose flour

1 package (¼ oz.) active dried yeast

1 teaspoon sea salt

1 egg, separated

1 teaspoon sugar

¾ cup lukewarm milk

1 tablespoon butter, for sautéing

To serve

crème fraîche or sour cream

caviar and/or salmon keta

herbs, such as snipped chives and dill sprigs

about 4 pieces smoked salmon, finely sliced

Makes 24

• You can buy cocktail blini in many supermarkets and delicatessens, but usually they're not made authentically with buckwheat flour.
• Store in an airtight container for up to 3 days.
• Reheat in the oven at 400°F for about 5 minutes.

Mix the flour, yeast, and salt in a bowl and make a hollow in the center. Beat the egg yolk with the sugar and ¾ cup warm water and add to the hollow. Mix well, then cover with a damp cloth and let rise at room temperature until doubled in size, about 2 hours.

Beat in the milk to make a thick, creamy batter. Cover again and leave for 1 hour until small bubbles appear on the surface.

Beat the egg white to soft peak stage, then fold it into the batter.

Heat a heavy skillet or crêpe pan and brush with butter. Drop in about 1 teaspoon of batter to make a pancake about 1 inch in diameter. Cook until the surface bubbles, about 2–3 minutes, then flip it over with a spatula and cook the second side for 2 minutes.

Put on a plate in the oven to keep warm while you cook the remaining blini. Don't put the blini on top of each other. Serve them warm.

To serve, top with a spoonful of crème fraîche or sour cream, snipped chives or dill sprigs, and a small pile of caviar or keta or a curl of smoked salmon.

Filling and delicious, **pizzas and pastries** can form the basis of the complete party menu.

homemade pizza bases

3½ cups unbleached white bread flour,
plus extra for dusting

2 teaspoons sea salt

½ package(¼ oz.) active dried yeast

1 tablespoon olive oil, plus extra for greasing

*2-inch plain cookie cutter and several baking trays,
well greased*

Makes 100 mini pizza bases Ⓥ

Mix the flour, salt, and yeast in a large bowl and make a
hollow in the center. Add 1¼ cups lukewarm water and the
oil. Gradually work the flour into the liquid to form a soft
but not sticky dough. If too dry, add extra lukewarm water,
1 tablespoon at a time. If too sticky, add extra flour,
1 tablespoon at a time.

Transfer to a lightly floured surface and knead for 10 minutes
until the dough is very elastic and smooth. Alternatively,
work for 5 minutes at low speed in a mixer fitted with dough
hooks. Transfer to a clean bowl dusted with flour, cover with
greased plastic wrap or a damp cloth and let rise at room
temperature until doubled in size—about 1 hour.

Punch down the risen dough, turn out, knead briefly, then
roll out to ⅛ inch thick. Stamp out rounds with the cookie
cutter. Arrange apart on the baking trays. With oiled fingers
press out each pizza round to 2¼ inches in diameter.

Add toppings of your choice and bake in a preheated oven
at 425°F for 10–15 minutes. Serve immediately.

You can also precook the bases at 425°F for 5 minutes, let
cool, then store in airtight containers for up to 2 days. Just
before serving, top and bake for 10–15 minutes.

Mini versions of your favorite Italian **pizzas** might have been especially designed for partying.

pizza toppings

Use a selection of Italian ingredients either homemade or store-bought. Don't use more than 3–4 ingredients on each pizza or the flavors will become too complicated.

• Red pesto brushed over the surface, then topped with a curl of grilled yellow bell pepper and half a garlic-spiked Oven-Dried Tomato (page 35) and sprinkled with fresh thyme leaves Ⓥ

• Bake the bases for 5 minutes, then top with a thick layer of Baba Ganoush or eggplant purée (page 40), then sprinkle with toasted pine nuts and cracked black pepper Ⓥ

• Fontina cheese with anchovy and a dot of red pesto

• Fontina cheese, pancetta strips, and cracked black pepper

• Grilled yellow bell pepper with roasted baby artichokes Ⓥ

• Oven-Dried Tomatoes (page 35) with olive oil or fontina and tarragon Ⓥ

• Grilled red bell pepper with fried fresh sage leaves Ⓥ

• Anchovies with melted mozzarella and dried oregano

• Onion Marmalade (page 48) with Oven-Dried Tomatoes (page 35) or cracked black pepper and sea salt Ⓥ

• Sautéed mushrooms with Gruyère, gorgonzola, and mozzarella Ⓥ

• Flaked fresh tuna with scallions and capers

• Grilled, finely sliced eggplant with Oven-Dried Tomatoes (page 35) and herbs. Ⓥ

tart pastry dough

1⅓ cups all-purpose flour

1 teaspoon sea salt

¼ teaspoon sugar

7 tablespoons unsalted butter, chilled and chopped

1 egg

1 tablespoon milk

a 2-inch plain or fluted cookie cutter

a deep 12-cup mini muffin pan, tartlet pans, or barquette (boat-shaped) molds, as many as possible

Makes about 34–36 mini tart shells or 18 barquettes ⓥ

This easy, basic pastry dough recipe can be used to make mini tart crusts of many kinds. If you want to make a larger quantity, make multiple batches—don't simply increase the quantities of ingredients. If you like making dough by hand, by all means use the traditional method. I don't, because preparing for a party is about minimizing time and effort so the excess can be used to make other dishes—and to have fun!

Put the flour, salt, and sugar in a food processor and pulse to mix. Add the butter and pulse until the mixture resembles fine crumbs. Put the egg and milk in a small bowl and beat lightly with a fork. Add to the food processor and pulse a few times, then process until the dough forms a ball. Wrap in plastic and chill for about 30 minutes or for up to 1 week.

mini tart crusts

Knead the chilled dough briefly to soften, then roll out on a lightly floured work surface to ⅛ inch thick. Cut out rounds with the cookie cutter. Gather the trimmings, reroll, and cut out more rounds. Cover with plastic wrap.

Put 1 round in each cup of the muffin cups and press into the corners to thin the dough around the edges and push it up the sides of the mold. Prick the bases with a fork. (Keep the remaining dough covered with plastic wrap.)

Bake in a preheated oven at 375°F for about 15 minutes until lightly golden. Remove from the oven, cool in the pan for a couple of minutes, then transfer to a wire rack to cool. Wipe the muffin pan clean and repeat until all the dough rounds have been cooked.

Fill with your choice of fillings on pages 62 and bake as directed.

- *Use immediately or store in airtight containers for up to 1 week.*
- *To freeze, open freeze in a single layer, transfer to freezer bags, seal, label, and keep frozen for up to 1 month.*
- *To use from frozen, reheat in a preheated oven at 375°F for 5 minutes. Let cool, then fill.*
- *To cook a filling in the tart shells from frozen, let thaw at room temperature for 20 minutes, then fill and bake according to your recipe.*

barquette crusts

Knead the chilled dough briefly to soften, then roll out on a lightly floured surface to ⅛-inch thick. Starting in one corner, put a barquette mold face-down on the dough. Using a sharp knife, cut around the mold leaving a ½-inch edge of dough all the way round. Press the dough cut-out into the mold, trimming the excess neatly. Repeat for the other barquette molds. Gather the trimmings, reroll, and cut out more barquette shapes.

Prick the base of each dough-lined mold with a fork, then chill for 30 minutes.

Cut out pieces of parchment paper to fit the shells, press into the shells to cover the dough, and fill with ceramic baking beans or rice. Stand the molds on a baking tray and bake blind in a preheated oven at 375°F for 15 minutes.

Remove the paper and beans and return to the oven for a further 5–10 minutes until lightly golden. Let cool in the molds for 2–3 minutes, then transfer to a wire rack to cool completely.

Wipe the molds clean and repeat using the remaining pastry dough.

- *Store and/or freeze, then thaw, fill, and bake as in the previous recipe.*

mini tarts and barquettes

36 tart crusts or 18 barquettes
(page 61)

Basic filling

1 egg

1 egg yolk

1 cup heavy cream

Asparagus and Prosciutto

2 tablespoons peanut oil

6 slices prosciutto,
sliced crosswise

1 onion, finely chopped

2–3 oz. asparagus tips

½ cup freshly grated
Parmesan cheese

Leek, Feta, and Black Olives Ⓥ

1 tablespoon butter or peanut oil

8 oz. baby leeks,
finely sliced crosswise

½ cup feta cheese, crumbled

½ cup black olives,
pitted and halved

**Blue Cheese, Pine Nuts,
and Basil** Ⓥ

½ cup pine nuts

⅔ cup blue cheese, such as
dolcellate, chopped

2–3 sprigs of basil

freshly cracked black pepper

*several baking sheets,
well greased*

**Makes 34–36 mini tarts
or 18 barquettes**

Prepare the tart crusts or barquettes. To make the basic filling, beat the egg, egg yolk, and cream together in a measuring cup with a lip.

Asparagus and Prosciutto

Heat the oil in a skillet, add the prosciutto, and sauté until crisp. Remove and drain on paper towels. Add the onion and stir-fry until softened and golden.

Meanwhile, steam or microwave the asparagus tips for 1–2 minutes until *al dente*. Chop into ½-inch pieces.

Divide the onions, asparagus, prosciutto, and Parmesan between the tart crusts, then pour in the basic filling mixture. Cook in a preheated oven at 350°F for 10 minutes or until the custard has set and the tops are golden. Remove from the oven, set aside for 5 minutes to firm the custard, then serve warm.

Leek, Feta, and Black Olives Ⓥ

Heat the butter or oil in a skillet, add the leeks, and sauté gently until softened and translucent. Divide the leeks, feta, and olives between the tart crusts, then pour in the egg mixture. Cook as for Asparagus and Prosciutto and serve warm.

Blue Cheese, Pine Nuts, and Basil Ⓥ

Heat a skillet, add the pine nuts, and stir-fry until golden. Divide the cheese between the tart crusts, add the egg mixture, top with pine nuts, and bake as before. Serve warm, topped with basil sprigs and cracked black pepper.

anchovy pinwheels

These simple savory cookies are delicious with anchovies, but you can try other variations, such as red pesto or tapenade.

2 oz. canned anchovies, finely chopped

1 lb. puff pastry, either fresh or frozen and thawed

beaten egg, to seal

several damp, nonstick baking trays

Makes about 60

• *The cooled pinwheels can be stored in an airtight container for up to 3 days.*

Using a mortar and pestle, mash the anchovies to a paste with 1 teaspoon water. Keep adding water until a smooth, brushable liquid results.

Roll out the pastry on a floured work surface to ⅛ inch thick.

Using a pastry brush, brush the anchovy mixture all over the surface (not too thick, or the taste will be too strong). Brush the far edge with beaten egg.

Starting at the edge nearest you, roll up the dough into a sausage about 1 inch thick, and press the egg-washed edge to seal. Chill for 30 minutes.

Cut the sausage crosswise into ⅛-inch thick slices and arrange flat and apart on damp, nonstick baking trays (sprinkle them with water if necessary).

Bake, in batches if necessary, in a preheated oven at 400°F for about 10–12 minutes until crisp and golden. Remove from the oven, let cool for 3 minutes, then transfer to a wire rack to cool completely.

spice-speckled cheese straws

Homemade cheese straws taste better than the bought variety, and are very easy to make.

1 cup all-purpose flour

½ teaspoon sea salt

1 teaspoon dry mustard powder

½ cup grated Cheddar cheese

2 tablespoons freshly grated Parmesan cheese

5 tablespoons butter, chilled and diced

1 egg yolk

juice of ½ lemon

paprika, for dusting (optional)

several baking trays, greased

Makes 36 Ⓥ

• *The cooled straws can be stored in an airtight container for up to 3 days.*

Put the flour, salt, mustard, and both cheeses in a food processor and pulse to mix. Add the butter and pulse until the mixture resembles fine crumbs.

Mix the egg yolk and lemon juice in a small pitcher, then pour into the processor with the motor running. Stop mixing when the mixture forms a ball, then transfer to a floured surface and knead briefly to form a ball.

Roll out to a rectangle about ⅛ inch thick. Using a hot, sharp knife, cut into strips 3 x ½ inch. Twist into spirals and arrange apart on baking trays.

Bake in a preheated oven at 350°F for 10 minutes until golden. Remove from the oven, dust with paprika if using, then cool on the baking tray.

Variation An easy version is to roll out store-bought puff pastry until very thin, sprinkle with freshly grated Parmesan cheese and mustard seeds, then fold over and roll again. Fold over loosely and cut into strips. Twist the strips into spirals and arrange apart on a greased baking tray. Press the ends down and bake as in the main recipe.

leaves and seaweed

Perfect with fingerfood, leaves
and seaweed add crunch and flavor
as well as natural wrapability
to other savory ingredients.

sushi rice

The major requirement is the right kind of rice—aromatic, Japanese sushi rice that sticks together inside the seaweed. Sushi rice is sold in large supermarkets and speciality food stores.

2 cups sushi rice

Sushi vinegar

⅔ cup Japanese rice vinegar

⅓ cup sugar

4 teaspoons sea salt

3 inches fresh ginger, peeled, grated, then squeezed in a garlic mincer

3 garlic cloves, crushed

Makes 2 sushi rolls, 6 slices each ⓥ

Wash the rice 5 times in cold water. Let drain in a strainer for at least 30 minutes, or overnight.

Put in a saucepan with 2⅓ cups water (the same volume of water plus 15 percent more). Cover tightly and bring to a boil over high heat. Reduce the heat to medium and boil for 10 minutes. Reduce to low and simmer for 5 minutes. Do not raise the lid. Still covered, let rest for 10 minutes.

Put the vinegar, sugar, salt, ginger, and garlic in a saucepan and heat gently.

Spread the rice over a wide dish, cut through with a rice paddle or wooden spoon, and fan to cool. Cut the vinegar mixture through the rice with the spoon.

Use immediately while still tepid. Do not chill—cold spoils sushi. (The rice contains vinegar, which will preserve it for a short time.)

The rice is now ready to be assembled in one of the recipes on the following pages. For a party, prepare at least 3 kinds, with one of each kind per person.

Variation Wipe 1 sheet of kombu seaweed with a cloth, then slash several times with a knife. Add to the rice cooking water. Bring slowly to a boil. Discard the seaweed just before boiling point.

cucumber sushi

This simple, traditional sushi is a favorite with vegetarians.

1 sheet nori seaweed, toasted

1 quantity sushi rice (page 70)

½ teaspoon wasabi paste

1 mini cucumber, seeded and sliced lengthwise

Makes 12 ⓥ

Cut the seaweed in half. Put one piece on a bamboo sushi mat, shiny side down. Divide the rice in half and press each portion into a cylinder shape. Put one cylinder in the middle of one piece of seaweed and press out the rice to meet the front edge. Press toward the far edge, leaving about ½–1 inch bare.

Brush ¼ teaspoon wasabi down the middle of the rice and put a line of cucumber on top.

Roll the mat gently from the front edge, pinch gently, then complete the roll and squeeze to make a tight cylinder. Make a second cylinder using the remaining ingredients.

The sushi can be wrapped in plastic and left like this until you are ready to cut and serve.

To serve, cut in half with a wet knife and trim off the end (optional—you may like to leave a "cockade" of cucumber sticking out the end). Cut each half in 3 and arrange on a serving platter. Small dishes of Japanese tamari soy sauce, pink pickled ginger, and wasabi paste are traditional accompaniments.

Note Sushi rice can be very sticky. To make it easier to handle, the Japanese use "hand vinegar"—a bowl of water with a splash of vinegar added.

sushi allsorts:
fillings and toppings

Use your choice of 1–5 of the ingredients listed below
and arrange them in a line across the rice 1 inch from
the front edge. If using more than 2 fillings, use a
whole sheet of seaweed instead of half. The roll is
completed and cut as in the previous recipe.

- Scallions, finely sliced lengthwise

- Carrots, finely sliced then blanched

- Daikon (mooli), finely sliced lengthwise

- Cucumber, seeded and sliced lengthwise

- Green beans or yard-long beans, blanched

- Red and/or yellow bell peppers, halved, seeded, and
sliced into strips

- Trout or salmon caviar

- Smoked fish, cut into long shreds

- Very fresh fish fillets, sliced and marinated in lime juice
or rice vinegar for 30 minutes

- Cooked shrimp, peeled, deveined, and halved lengthwise

- Raw or grilled tuna, finely sliced

- Three eggs, beaten, cooked as a very thin omelet, then
finely sliced

- Baby spinach leaves, blanched

- Avocado, finely sliced lengthwise.

sushi cones

4 sheets nori seaweed, halved
(7 x 4 inches) and toasted

2 quantities cooked sushi rice (page 70)

Fillings such as

enoki mushrooms

raw or smoked salmon

blanched asparagus

finely sliced carrot

cucumber strips

thin omelet, sliced

sesame seeds

wasabi

pickled ginger

Makes 8

Put a sheet of nori, shiny side down, on
a work surface. Put 1 tablespoon rice on
the left edge. Using wet hands, spread it
lightly to cover one half of the seaweed
completely. Add your choice of filling
ingredients diagonally across the rice,
letting them overlap the top left corner.

To roll the cones, put one finger in the
middle of the bottom edge, then roll up
the cone from the bottom left, using
your finger as the axis of the turn. As
each cone is made, put it on a serving
platter with the seam down.

seafood sushi

2 sheets nori seaweed, toasted

1 quantity cooked sushi rice (page 70)

Toppings such as

about ¾ cup smoked salmon

salmon, or trout caviar

cooked seafood or fresh raw fish

Makes 12

Make 2 sushi rolls as in the previous recipe, using whole sheets of seaweed rather than halves. Do not add filling. When the rolls are made, pat them into rectangular cylinders. Cut each one into 6 and pat into tidy rectangles. Top each one with a spoonful of keta (salmon caviar) or pieces of seafood or fish cut to size.

thai crab salad
in endive leaves

2 red chiles, cored, seeded and
finely chopped

1 garlic clove, minced

2 inches lemongrass, very finely chopped

grated zest and juice of 1 lime

1 tablespoon fish sauce

½ cup canned coconut milk

1 teaspoon sugar

1 small onion or shallot, finely chopped,
or 2 scallions, finely sliced·

sea salt, to taste

3½ cups cooked crabmeat or
shelled, deveined shrimp, finely chopped

1 bunch basil, preferably Asian basil, torn

1 bunch cilantro leaves, torn, plus extra
to serve

Belgian endive leaves, preferably red,
or mini romaine lettuce leaves, to serve

Makes about 24 filled leaves

Put 1 chopped chile, the garlic,
lemongrass, lime zest and juice, fish
sauce, coconut milk, and sugar in a bowl
and mix well until the sugar dissolves.
Stir in the onion, shallot, or scallion.
Taste and adjust the seasoning.

Fold in the crabmeat or chopped shrimp
and herbs, then pile about 1 tablespoon
in the base of each endive leaf or lettuce
leaf. Serve topped with finely chopped
chile and torn cilantro leaves.

hummus salad
in crisp leaves

1 quantity homemade or store-bought
hummus

4 mini cucumbers or 1 large cucumber, halved,
seeded, and finely diced

3 ripe red tomatoes, seeded and finely diced

1 red Spanish onion, finely chopped

3 tablespoons chopped fresh mint leaves

3 tablespoons chopped fresh cilantro leaves

To serve

24 Belgian endive or baby lettuce leaves

sprigs of cilantro

grated zest of 1–2 lemons

Makes about 24 leaves ⓥ

Put the hummus in a bowl, then fold
in the cucumber, tomatoes, onion, mint,
and cilantro leaves.

Put 1 tablespoon in each endive or
lettuce leaf, arrange on a platter, and
serve topped with a sprig of cilantro and
grated lemon zest.

Belgian endive and mini lettuce **leaves** make perfect bite-size edible spoons.

leaf scoop fillings

Quick, easy, and delicious fingerfood containers, leaves can be filled with one of the recipes in this section, others from this book—or use one of your own favorite mixtures. Any good gourmet store will provide lots of other delicious possibilities. Listed here are just a few serving ideas.

Your choice of

• Smoked chicken with Mexican Salsa (page 40), shown opposite

• Shredded turkey and cranberry sauce with cress, shown opposite

• Baba Ganoush eggplant purée (page 40) sprinkled with chopped parsley and toasted sesame seeds, shown opposite Ⓥ

• Soft goat cheese rolled into balls with a spoonful of salmon or trout caviar, plus pepper and lemon zest, shown opposite

• Vietnamese Pork Balls (page 102) with Nuòc Cham (page 119)

• Soft goat cheese mixed with chopped herbs Ⓥ

• Smoked salmon and sour cream

• Onion and garlic sautéed in butter or olive oil until almost melted, then mixed with ricotta Ⓥ

• Felafel (page 106) with hummus, harissa, and mint Ⓥ

• Bocconcini cheeses, halved and topped with red pesto. Ⓥ

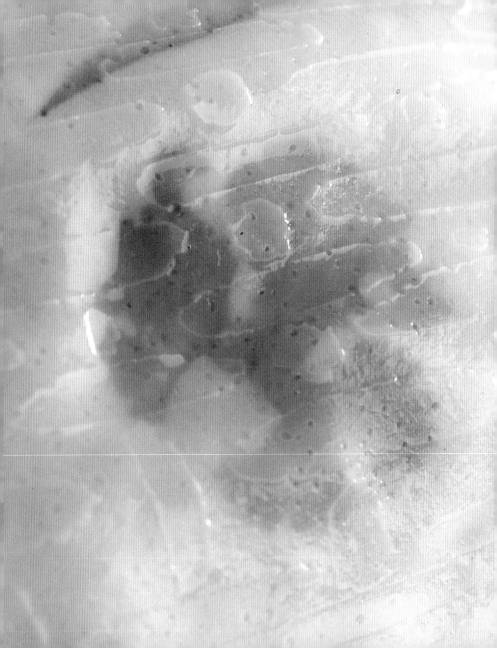

wraps and pockets

Convenient containers for party food, wraps and pockets can be used with specially cooked fillings, store-bought goodies, or other recipes in this book.

ciabatta pockets with rare roast beef, wasabi mayonnaise, and baby salad

These pockets are crisp and delicious. Use ciabatta rolls, halved, or the ends of loaves (use the middles to make bruschetta). Other fillings can also be used, such as the Frikadelle (page 101) or Vietnamese Pork Balls (page 102).

2 lb. beef fillet, in the piece

2 tablespoons olive oil

12 ciabatta rolls, halved

butter, for spreading (optional)

baby salad leaf mixture

sea salt and freshly ground black pepper

Wasabi mayonnaise

1 egg

1 egg yolk

1 garlic clove, crushed

1 tablespoon lemon juice

sea salt

peanut or sunflower oil (see method)

1 tablespoon wasabi paste or freshly grated horseradish

Makes 24

• *Do not use bottled mayo—better to choose another dressing altogether!*

To roast the beef, heat a heavy ovenproof skillet or roasting pan on top of the stove, then add the olive oil and swirl to coat the surface.

Add the whole fillet of beef and fry at high heat on all sides until well browned—about 5 minutes. Remove from the heat. You can prepare the beef in advance to this point.

Preheat the oven to its highest temperature, but at least 400°F. Put the beef, still in its skillet or pan, into the oven and roast 15–20 minutes. Remove from the oven and set aside in a warm place to set the juices. Let cool.

Cut the beef crosswise into ⅛-inch slices, then into strips suitable for stuffing the rolls. (Thicker slices taste better, don't be skimpy!) Cover with plastic.

To make the wasabi mayonnaise, put the egg, egg yolk, garlic, lemon juice, and salt in a small blender or food processor and blend until pale. Add the oil, drop by drop at first, then faster, in stages, to form a thick emulsion. If the mixture becomes too thick, add a tablespoon of warm water. Add the wasabi paste or horseradish and pulse to mix.

Cut the ciabatta rolls in half and make a pocket in each half by pressing with your fingers. Add a smear of butter, if using. Put a pinch of salad leaves in the pocket, 1–2 strips of roast beef, then top with a teaspoon of wasabi mayonnaise.

Variation This combination is also good as a topping for Danish Open Sandwiches (page 50).

2 potatoes, finely chopped

1 carrot, finely chopped

1 cup peanut oil

1 small onion, chopped

¼ teaspoon nigella
(onion seeds) (optional)

1 cup corn kernels,
fresh or frozen

¼ cup shelled peas

4 oz. paneer or
mozzarella cheese

1 tablespoon
chopped cilantro

2 red chiles, halved, seeded,
and chopped

a pinch of chile powder
(optional)

1 teaspoon amchoor
(mango powder)
or lime juice

½ teaspoon sea salt

15 sheets ready-made
phyllo pastry

melted butter, for brushing

Makes 30 Ⓥ

• *Paneer is sold in some large
supermarkets and Asian
stores. To make your own, see
recipe on page 28.*
• *To prepare the samosas
ahead, cook the day before,
cool and chill. Reheat at 350°F
for about 10 minutes just
before serving.*

indian samosas

Freshly cooked and utterly delicious, vegetarian samosas are sold at roadside stalls and railroad stations all over India and Pakistan. A great hit at fashionable parties in Bombay and Delhi, these smaller versions are made with phyllo rather than traditional pastry, and rolled into triangles rather than cones. Samosas are usually deep-fried, but can also be oven-baked.

To make the filling, cook the potatoes and carrots in boiling salted water until just cooked, about 3–5 minutes. Drain.

Heat 3 tablespoons of the oil in a wok or saucepan and stir-fry the onion and nigella until the onions are softened and translucent. Add the potatoes, carrot, corn, and peas and stir-fry for 1 minute.

Stir in the cheese, cilantro, chiles, chile powder, if using, amchoor or lime juice, and salt. Let cool.

Unwrap the phyllo pastry and put 1 sheet on a work surface. Keep the rest covered with a damp cloth while you work. Cut the sheet of pastry in half and brush the sheets all over with melted butter, fold each half into 3, lengthwise, buttering between, making 2 long strips.

Put 1 tablespoon filling at one corner of pastry. Fold the corner over to form a triangle. Continue folding until the filling is enclosed and the whole strip of pastry has been used. Repeat until all the pastry and filling have been used.

When all the samosas are made, heat the remaining oil to 375°F in a wok or saucepan. Add 2–3 samosas at a time and fry until golden, turning them once.

As each one is cooked, remove and drain on paper towels, then serve hot, warm, or cool.

Variation To bake the samosas, space them apart on a lightly greased baking tray, brush with a mixture of peanut oil and melted butter. Bake in a preheated oven at 350°F for 15 minutes until crisp and golden.

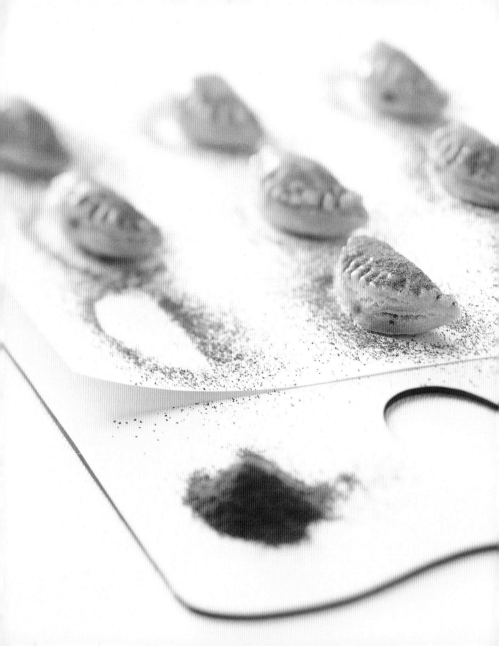

empanaditas

India has samosas, England has Cornish pasties—but Mexico and South America have one of the most delicious of all pastry packages, the empanada. Empanaditas, the little ones, are perfect as fingerfood. They are usually made with corn tortilla dough and deep-fried, but to save time, you might like to use ready-rolled puff pastry, then cook them in the oven.

2 cups lean ground beef

1 onion, finely chopped

1 garlic clove, minced

1 tablespoon finely chopped parsley

sea salt and freshly ground black pepper

1 cup tomato purée

⅓ cup raisins, soaked in water

¼ cup slivered almonds, toasted

⅓ cup dry sherry

1 lb. puff pastry, fresh or frozen and thawed

paprika or mild chile powder, for dusting (optional)

Mexican Salsa or Chile Mojo (page 40–41), to serve

a cookie cutter, 3 inches in diameter

baking sheets

Makes about 40

Heat a non-stick skillet, add the meat, and sauté, stirring from time to time, for about 30 minutes, or until browned. Add the onion and garlic, stir-fry for 2 minutes, then add the parsley, salt, pepper, tomato purée, raisins, and almonds. Stir-fry until the mixture thickens. Remove from the heat and stir in the sherry. Set aside to develop the flavors.

Roll out the puff pastry to about ⅛ inch thick, then cut out rounds using the cookie cutter. Reroll and cut the trimmings.

Put 1 tablespoon of filling in each circle, slightly off-center. Fold the pastry in half and press the edges with a fork to seal. Chill for 30 minutes.

Arrange apart on baking trays and cook in a preheated oven at 375°F for 15–20 minutes until browned.

Sprinkle with paprika or mild chile powder if using, then serve with a Mexican Salsa or Chile Mojo.

fresh vietnamese spring rolls

24 small Vietnamese ricepaper wrappers (6 inches)

1 oz. beanthread (cellophane) noodles (1 small bundle), soaked in boiling water for 20 minutes, drained, then snipped into 2-inch lengths

3 carrots, finely sliced into matchstick strips, preferably on a mandoline

1 mini cucumber, halved, seeded, and finely sliced into matchstick strips

6 scallions, halved then finely sliced lengthwise

2 baskets enoki mushrooms

fresh mint leaves

fresh cilantro leaves

1 small package fresh bean sprouts, trimmed, rinsed, and dried

2 cups cooked crabmeat, peeled, chopped shrimp, or stir-fried ground pork

Nuòc Cham dipping sauce, to serve (page 119)

Makes 24

• The wrappers come in packs of 50 large or 100 small. Wrap leftover wrappers in 2 layers of plastic and seal well. Leftover filling can made into balls or patties, sautéed, and served with toothpicks.

Vietnamese food is full of flavor and not as oily as Chinese. These fresh spring rolls are delicious. They can be made several hours in advance, then sprayed with a mist of water and covered with plastic wrap to prevent them from drying out. Children love to make them, so enlist their help.

Assemble all the ingredients on platters and fill a wide bowl with hot water. Work on one roll at a time.

Dip 1 ricepaper sheet in the water for about 30 seconds until softened. Put on a plate (not a board, which will dry out the ricepaper).

Put a small pinch of each ingredient in a line down the middle of the sheet, fold over both sides of the sheet, then roll up like a cigar. (If folding only one side, as shown, let some of the ingredients protrude from the other end.)

Spray with a mist of water and set aside on a plate, covered with a damp cloth, while you prepare the others.

To serve, spray with water again and serve with the dipping sauce—it's better to serve a small quantity at a time, in case they dry out.

Variation Stir 1 tablespoon sesame oil through the noodles after soaking.

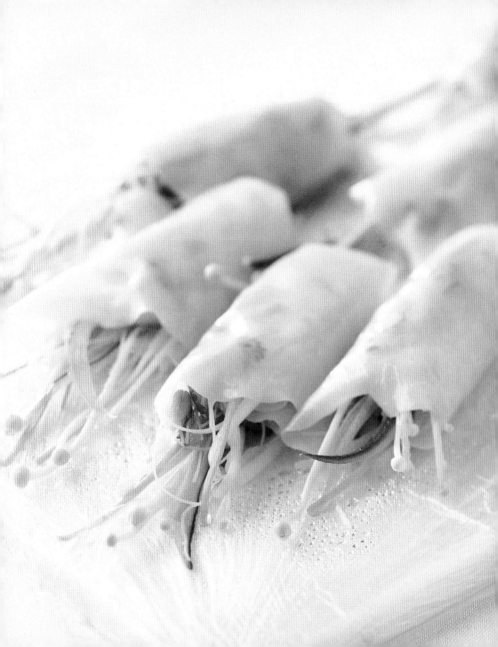

mini tortilla wraps

2 large mild chiles, seeded and halved lengthwise

4 cooked chicken breasts

2 roasted yellow bell peppers, sliced

20 small flour tortillas

4 Oven-Dried Tomatoes (page 35)

1 romaine lettuce, finely sliced

1 cup grated Cheddar or queso fresco cheese

leaves from 1 large bunch cilantro, torn

lime juice, to sprinkle

sea salt and freshly ground black pepper

Makes 40

Tortilla wraps can be made with any number of filling combinations. For a party, however, it's always a good idea to include something for vegetarians—I like avocado.

Pan-toast or grill the chiles until the skin is blistered. Scrape off the skin, then finely slice the chiles.

Pull the chicken breasts apart into long shreds.

Warm the tortillas, one by one, under the broiler for about 1 minute until they soften and puff slightly.

Arrange on a work surface and add a layer of each ingredient in a line across the tortilla, leaving about about 1 inch clear on one side. Sprinkle with lime juice, salt, and pepper. Fold up the side edge, then roll into a cylinder. Cut in half crosswise, then serve, seam-side down, or tied in a napkin.

chicken souvlaki

4 chicken breasts, boneless pork chops or lamb leg chops

sea salt

Marinade

4 garlic cloves, crushed

1 tablespoon fresh lemon juice

1 teaspoon cumin seeds, toasted in a dry skillet, then crushed with a mortar and pestle

1 teaspoon freshly ground black pepper

2 tablespoons extra virgin olive oil

To serve

1 package soft Middle Eastern flatbread, such as lavash, village bread, or pita

1 cup hummus

1 cup tabbouleh salad (page 97), store-bought or homemade

hot pepper sauce (optional)

6 scallions, cut into strips lengthwise, then blanched in boiling water

Serves about 24

All the components for this delicious wrap can be assembled in advance, then wrapped and cut just before serving. Roast lamb or pork can be used instead of the chicken. Make sure the chicken and breads are warm before assembling—wrap in napkins or serve as here, in packages.

Trim the chicken, pork, or lamb. Mix the marinade ingredients in a shallow non-metal dish, then add the chicken or meat and turn until well covered. Chill for 20 minutes or overnight to develop the flavors.

To cook the chicken, brush a heavy skillet with oil, add the drained chicken breasts, and sauté gently on each side until tender, about 15 minutes. Cook the pork gently until cooked through. Cook the lamb at high heat for about 10 minutes on each side until crisp outside and pink inside. Remove from the heat, let rest for 10 minutes, then cut into ⅙-inch strips. Sprinkle with salt, cover, and set aside until ready to assemble (reheat if necessary).

To assemble, cut the flatbread into pieces about 4 inches square. Heat the pieces briefly, then put a heaped teaspoon of hummus in the middle, add 1 tablespoon tabbouleh, some sliced chicken or meat, and a dab of hot pepper sauce, if using. Roll up the bread into a square package, folding over each end to enclose the filling. Tie up with the strips of scallion.

mini pita pockets

24 mini pita breads, or
12 medium ones, halved

tabbouleh salad (below),
or parsley sprigs

24 small slices of roast lamb
or chicken, 24 felafel (page 106)
or 24 cubes of cheese, such as
paneer or feta

2–3 red onions, finely sliced

about 2 cups tahini sauce
or hummus

hot pepper sauce, to taste
(optional)

Serves 24

Although pita breads are from the Middle East,
the nicest I ever had were in Pakistan—delicious
mini half-moons filled with crusty roast lamb, mild
red onion rings, and tahini sauce. Make these
with other kinds of fillings such as chicken, duck,
or Indian Cheese (page 28).

Gently warm the pita breads and cut in half
crosswise if large.

Split them open and add a spoonful of tabbouleh,
salad, or parsley, a few shreds of roast lamb,
chicken, felafel or cheese, a few onion rings, a
spoonful of tahini sauce or hummus, and a drop of
hot pepper sauce, if using.

Serve stacked in baskets or folded in cocktail napkins.

tabbouleh

½ cup toasted buckwheat

2 large ripe tomatoes

a large bunch of parsley

a large bunch of mint

3 scallions

2 tablespoons olive oil

1 tablespoon lemon juice

sea salt and cracked black pepper

Serves 24

Soak the buckwheat in water for 20 minutes, then
drain. Skin, deseed and chop the tomatoes. Chop
the parsley and mint. Finely chop the scallions.
Put the buckwheat, tomatoes, parsley, mint, and
scallions in a bowl, then toss with the olive oil,
lemon juice, a pinch of salt, and lots of cracked
black pepper.

bites and balls

A collection of delicious bites and balls from around the world. Serve them with toothpicks and a dipping sauce—or in pocket breads, on toast, in endive or lettuce leaves, or wrapped in tortillas.

frikadelle

These delicious meatballs are a traditional dish in Scandinavia, Holland, and Germany.

⅓ cup mashed potato

8 oz. ground beef

4 oz. ground veal

4 oz. ground lamb

½ cup dried breadcrumbs

⅓ cup light cream

1 egg, beaten

a pinch of freshly grated nutmeg

1 canned anchovy fillet, mashed

a pinch of ground allspice

sea salt and freshly ground black pepper

3 tablespoons butter

1 small onion, finely chopped

2 tablespoons vegetable oil

rosemary sprigs, for serving

Makes about 30

• The traditional meat combination is 8 oz. each of ground pork and veal.

Put the potato in a bowl with the meat, breadcrumbs, cream, egg, nutmeg, anchovy, allspice, a large pinch of salt, and a good grinding of black pepper. Mix well.

Heat 1 tablespoon of the butter in a skillet, add the onion, and sauté until softened and translucent. Stir into the meat mixture.

Wet your hands, take 1 tablespoon of the mixture, roll it between your palms to form a ball, then flatten it slightly. Repeat until all the mixture has been used. Arrange the balls apart on a tray, cover with plastic wrap, and chill for about 1 hour.

Heat the remaining butter and the oil in a heavy skillet, then sauté the meatballs, spaced apart, in batches, until browned on both sides. Shake them from time to time. Remove and drain on paper towels.

Serve with toothpicks or rosemary sprigs—the rosemary gives wonderful fragrance to the frikadelle.

Alternatively, serve with a Chile Dipping Sauce (page 102), or in mini hamburger buns, in pita breads (page 97), as Souvlaki (page 94), in tortilla wraps (page 93), or in ciabatta pockets (page 85) with your choice of salad leaves and sauce.

vietnamese pork balls with chile dipping sauce

1 lb. ground pork

6 garlic cloves, crushed

2 stalks lemongrass, finely sliced

1 bunch cilantro, finely chopped

2 fresh red chiles, seeded and chopped

1 tablespoon brown sugar

1 tablespoon Asian fish sauce

1 egg, beaten

sea salt and freshly ground black pepper

peanut oil, for frying

Chile dipping sauce

½ cup white rice vinegar

2–6 small or 1 large red chile, finely sliced

1 tablespoon fish sauce

1 scallion, finely sliced (optional)

½–1 tablespoon brown sugar

Makes about 12

A delicious traditional recipe that's perfect for a cocktail party. The original is manna from heaven to the dedicated chile-head. I am not, and find this amount is plenty. Don't just up the chile because you love it—remember some people don't. And of course they'll drink more to cool the fires, never realizing that water or alcohol won't help soothe a chile burn (only milk or yogurt will, in case you're interested!).Use fat Fresno chiles for a mild flavor, or tiny bird's eye chiles for blinding heat.

Mix all the ingredients for the chile dipping sauce in a small bowl, stir to dissolve the sugar, then set aside to develop the flavors.

To make the pork balls, put all the remaining ingredients except the peanut oil in a bowl and mix well. Dip your hands in water, take 1–2 tablespoons of the mixture, and roll it into a ball. Repeat with the remaining mixture. Put the balls, spaced apart, on a plate as you finish them. Chill for at least 30 minutes.

Fill a wok one-third full of peanut oil and heat to 375°F or until a cube of bread browns in 30 seconds. Add the pork balls, 6 at a time, and fry in batches until golden brown. Remove and drain on paper towels, keeping them warm in the oven until all the balls are done. Serve with the chile dipping sauce or Nuòc Cham (page 119).

thai crabcakes with chile dipping sauce

3 red chiles, seeded

3 scallions, finely sliced

2 garlic cloves, crushed

4 cilantro stalks, finely chopped

1 inch fresh ginger or galangal, chopped

6 kaffir lime leaves, finely sliced, or grated zest of 2 limes

1 tablespoon fish sauce

8 oz. boneless fish fillets, such as cod

1½ cups crabmeat (fresh, frozen, or canned)

2 Chinese long beans or 12 beans, finely sliced

1 oz. beanthread (cellophane) noodles (1 small bundle)

1 egg, beaten

2 tablespoons peanut oil, for frying

chile dipping sauce (page 102)

Makes about 30

Everyone loves Thai fishcakes and crabcakes. Chopped green beans or chopped asparagus are popular with western chefs, but I prefer snake beans (Chinese long beans)—they have better texture and a more interesting taste.

Put the chiles, scallions, garlic, cilantro stalks, ginger or galangal, kaffir lime leaves or lime zest, and fish sauce in a food processor and work to a paste. Add the fish and work to a paste. Transfer to a bowl and mix in the crabmeat and beans.

Soak the beanthread noodles in a bowl of hot water for 5 minutes, then drain and snip into short pieces, about 1 inch long. Mix into the fish and stir in the beaten egg. Wet your hands with water and shape the mixture into flat hamburger-shaped patties of 1–2 tablespoons each.

Heat the oil in a wok or skillet and swirl to coat the sides. Add the crabcakes, 3 at a time, and sauté until golden. Transfer to a plate lined with paper towels and keep them hot in the oven while you cook the remaining crabcakes. Serve with chile dipping sauce.

Note The crabcakes can also be deep-fried in a wok about one-third full of oil.

felafel

1 cup dried chickpeas
1 cup dried fava beans
1 large bunch parsley, chopped
3 tablespoons chopped fresh mint
½ cup bulgar wheat, soaked in hot water to cover for 15 minutes
4 garlic cloves, minced
1 egg
1 teaspoon ground cumin (optional)
1 teaspoon cardamom seeds, freshly crushed, or 1 teaspoon ground coriander
½ teaspoon baking soda
sea salt and freshly ground black pepper
3 scallions, chopped
1 leek, white only, or 1 onion chopped
1 red bell pepper, seeded and chopped
about ¼ cup sesame seeds
peanut or safflower oil, for frying
sprigs of cilantro, to serve

Makes about 20 Ⓥ

Serving Suggestions
• *Serve with toothpicks and a dip from pages 40–41.*
• *Serve in halved mini pita breads (page 97) with salad and hummus.*
• *Serve in mini lettuce leaves with a spoonful of hummus and a sprig of mint (page 78).*

Felafel are perfect for vegetarian guests—if the carnivores don't eat them all first.

Soak the dried chickpeas and broad beans overnight in water to cover. Drain.

Working in batches if necessary, put the chickpeas and fava beans in a food processor. Add the parsley, mint, bulgar wheat, garlic, egg, ground cumin, cardamom, baking soda, salt, and pepper. Pulse until coarsely blended. Transfer to a bowl.

Put the scallions, leek or onion, and red bell pepper in the food processor and pulse briefly until very finely chopped. Tip the bean mixture back into the food processor and pulse to mix. (Work in batches if necessary).

Set aside for 15 minutes, then chill for 30 minutes.

Moisten your hands and pinch off pieces of bean mixture about 1-inch diameter. Shape into balls with your hands. Spread the sesame seeds on a small plate and roll half the balls in the seeds, pressing them into the surface. Leave the other half plain.

Pour 1¼-inch depth of oil into a large skillet or wok. Heat to 370°F or until a cube of bread browns in 30 seconds. Cook in batches until brown, about 2 minutes, turning after 1 minute. Drain on paper towels, then serve topped with cilantro.

wontons
and satays

Delicious, bite-sized morsels, wontons and satays make perfect fingerfood, and many can be prepared ahead of time.

chinese moneybags

10 oz. ground pork or chicken

⅓ cup shelled shrimp (optional)

2 slices bacon, chopped

1 teaspoon crushed Szechuan peppercorns or freshly ground black pepper

1 egg white

1 teaspoon sesame oil

2 garlic cloves, crushed

1 inch fresh ginger, grated

a pinch of sea salt

6 scallions, white and green parts, finely sliced

4 canned water chestnuts, finely chopped

4 Chinese long beans or 12 green beans, finely sliced

2 packages small wonton wrappers

dipping sauce such as soy sauce, chile sauce, or Nuòc Cham (page 119), to serve

a cookie cutter or kitchen shears

Makes about 40

• *Packages vary, but usually contain about 40 large (5-inch) or 70 small (4-inch) wrappers. Leftover wrappers can be frozen.*

Put the pork or chicken, shrimp, if using, and bacon in a food processor and blend to a purée. Add the pepper, egg white, sesame oil, garlic, ginger, and salt and blend again.

Put all the remaining ingredients except the wonton wrappers and dipping sauce in a bowl, add the meat mixture, and mix well. Cover and chill while you prepare the wrappers.

Using a cookie cutter or kitchen shears, cut the wrappers into circles.

Put 1 tablespoon of the filling in the middle of each circle and spread the mixture almost to the edges. Put the circle on the palm of your hand and cup your hand, pressing down the filling with a spatula: you will achieve an open bag with a pleated top. Tap the base gently on the work surface to make a flat bottom, then neaten the pleated tops with your fingers. Repeat until all the moneybags are made.

Line several layers of a steamer, preferably bamboo, with banana leaves or parchment paper. Put the steamers, in tiers if preferred, in a wok, pour in boiling water to come just below the base of the steamer, cover, and steam until done, 7–10 minutes. Add extra boiling water as necessary.

Serve the moneybags, still in the steaming racks, with one or more small dishes of dipping sauce. Put the next batch of steamers on to cook while you serve the first batch.

vietnamese
mini spring rolls

1 oz. beanthread (cellophane) noodles (1 small bundle)

5 Chinese dried cloud ear mushrooms or fresh button mushrooms, finely diced

8 oz. ground pork

½ onion, finely chopped

3 garlic cloves, crushed

3 scallions, finely sliced

¼ cup crabmeat (fresh, frozen, or canned and drained) or finely chopped shrimp

sea salt and freshly ground black pepper

1 package large Vietnamese ricepaper wrappers (50 sheets)

peanut or safflower oil, for frying

To serve (optional)

mini lettuce leaves, such as Little Gem

grated carrot

sprigs of basil

sprigs of cilantro

Nuòc Cham dipping sauce (page 119)

Makes about 40 mini rolls

• *The wrappers come in packs of 50 large or 100 small. Wrap leftover wrappers in 2 layers of plastic and seal well. Leftover filling can be made into balls or patties, sautéed, and served with toothpicks.*

You can make spring rolls in advance, then freeze and deep-fry them from frozen—or deep-fry in advance, then reheat in the oven before serving.

Soak the noodles in hot water for 20 minutes. Drain and snip into short lengths. Soak the dried mushrooms in boiling water to cover for 30 minutes, then drain and chop. Put the noodles, mushrooms, pork, onion, garlic, scallions, crabmeat, salt, and pepper in a food processor and pulse to mix.

Put 4 ricepapers in a bowl of warm water and let soften for 1–2 minutes. Cut each one into 4 segments. Put 1 segment on a work surface, put 1 teaspoon of filling next to the curved edge, and pat the filling into a small cylinder. Fold the curved edge over the filling, fold over the 2 sides like an envelope, then roll up towards the long pointed end. Press to seal. Repeat with all the other wrappers.

Fill a wok one-third full of peanut oil and heat to 375°F or until a piece of noodle fluffs up immediately. Put 5–6 spring rolls in the oil and fry until crisp and golden. Remove and drain on paper towels. Repeat until all the spring rolls are cooked.

Serve plain, or in baby lettuce leaves with grated carrot, basil, and cilantro sprigs. Nuòc Cham is the traditional dipping sauce.

Variation Try the fresh, uncooked Spring Rolls on page 90.

crispy pork wontons

Crunchy wontons produce lots of pizzazz for very little effort. Instead of this pork filling, try chicken, crab, or chopped shrimp.

8 oz. ground pork

4 garlic cloves, minced

4 water chestnuts, chopped

4 scallions, white and green parts halved lengthwise, then sliced crosswise

1 package small wonton wrappers

1 egg, beaten with a drop of water

peanut or safflower oil

sea salt and freshly ground black pepper

soy sauce or Nuòc Cham (page 119), to serve

Makes about 40

• *The wontons can be deep-fried, then cooled and frozen. Reheat from frozen for 15 minutes in a preheated oven at 300°F before serving.*

• *The wontons can be assembled and frozen before cooking, but if so, make sure the meat has never been frozen before.*

• *They can also be cooked early in the day of the party, then cooled quickly and refrigerated until ready to serve. Reheat for 10 minutes in a preheated oven at 400°F.*

Put the pork in a bowl with the garlic, water chestnuts, scallions, salt, and pepper and mix well, using your hands or a spoon.

Take the wonton wrappers out of the plastic bag, but keep them covered with a damp cloth or the plastic as you work, because they can dry out quickly.

Put 1 wrapper on the work surface and put about ½ tablespoon of filling in the middle. Brush a circle of beaten egg around the filling. Pull up the sides of the wrapper and twirl or press it together to form a "waist." Open out the top of the wrapper to form a frill. Repeat until all the wontons are made.

Fill a wok one-third full of peanut or sunflower oil and heat to 375°F. To test, drop in a fragment of wonton wrapper—it should fluff up immediately when the oil is the right temperature.

Working in batches, add the wontons 3–4 at a time and fry for a few minutes on each side until brown and crisp. Don't let the oil get too hot, or the dough will cook before the filling.

As each batch is complete, transfer to a plate covered with paper towels (skim debris off the oil between batches).

Serve hot, with plain soy sauce or Nuòc Cham.

middle eastern lamb boats

The filling for these delicious little morsels should be well seasoned, before and after cooking.

1 tablespoon peanut safflower oil, plus extra for greasing

1 package pine nuts, about 3–4 oz.

8 oz. ground lamb or beef

1 onion, grated

1 garlic clove, minced

¼ cup chopped fresh parsley

1 lb. ready-made shortcrust pastry dough

1 egg, beaten with water, to glaze

sea salt and freshly ground black pepper

To serve (optional)

finely chopped fresh parsley

sea salt flakes

several baking trays, greased

Makes 150

Heat the oil in a skillet, add the pine nuts, and stir-fry them quickly until golden, about 30 seconds.

Put the meat, onion, garlic, parsley, pine nuts, salt, and pepper in a bowl and mix well. Set aside.

Roll out the dough to about ⅛ inch thick. Using a long ruler and a sharp knife, trim the edges straight, then cut the dough into long strips about 1 inch wide, then across to make squares. Cover the dough while you make up the boats.

Brush egg glaze down two opposite sides of the square, then put about ½ teaspoon of filling in the middle of the square. Fold in half, with the glazed edges together, place on the work surface with the open side upward. Widen the opening to show the filling and make a boat shape, then tap the boat on the work surface to flatten the bottom. Pinch up the prow and stern to force up the filling.

Put the boats close together in a single layer on greased baking trays. Bake in a preheated oven at 350°F for about 45 minutes or until golden brown and still moist.

Serve immediately, sprinkled with parsley and sea salt flakes, if using.

Sticks and skewers are an efficient way to serve fingerfood.

lemongrass sticks

2 tablespoons peanut oil

1½ lb. ground chicken

1 cup desiccated coconut, soaked for 30 minutes in 1 cup boiling water, then drained

1 large red chile, seeded, and finely chopped

2 tablespoons brown sugar

grated zest of 1 lime

sea salt and freshly ground black pepper

10–20 lemongrass stalks, either whole or halved lengthwise, or satay sticks

Spice paste

12 Thai shallots or 1 regular shallot, sliced

6 garlic cloves, sliced

2 red chiles, seeded, and sliced

1 inch fresh ginger, peeled and chopped

1 teaspoon turmeric powder

2 teaspoons coriander seeds, crushed

1 teaspoon black peppercorns, crushed

6 almonds, crushed

1 tablespoon fish sauce

2 cloves, crushed

10–20 bamboo skewers, soaked in cold water for 30 minutes

Makes about 20

The chicken mixture can be cooked on other kinds of skewers, but the lemongrass gives delicious flavor. You can buy ready-made Thai curry pastes, but the recipe given here is especially delicious. The lemongrass infuses the meat with delicate fragrance.

Put all the spice paste ingredients in a grinder and blend to paste. Alternatively, use a mortar and pestle.

Heat the oil in a small skillet, add the paste, and sauté for about 5 minutes. Cool, then put in a bowl with the chicken, coconut, chopped chiles, sugar, lime zest, salt, and pepper. Mix well.

Take 2 tablespoons of the mixture and mold onto the end of the lemongrass stalks or satay skewers. Wrap the ends of the stalks in little squares of foil to stop them burning.

Cook on a grill or under the broiler until cooked and golden—5–10 minutes, then serve with a dip such as Nuòc Cham.

Vietnamese Nuòc Cham is a delicious, piquant, salty, spicy condiment used as an all-purpose dipping sauce. Crush 2 garlic cloves, 1 seeded red chile, and 1 tablespoon sugar to a paste, using a spice grinder or mortar and pestle. Add ½ chopped lime and any collected juice and purée again. Stir in 1½ tablespoons fish sauce and about 125 ml water, then serve in small dipping bowls.

yakitori

10 chicken thighs, bones removed, skin intact, cut into 1-inch cubes (about 3 pieces per thigh)

10 scallions or baby leeks, halved lengthwise, then cut into ½-inch lengths

4 fresh shiitake mushrooms or white mushrooms, cut into ½-inch squares

4 red or yellow bell peppers, cored, seeded, and cut into ½-inch squares

Japanese 7-spice or crushed black pepper

Yakitori sauce

2 cups soy sauce

1 cup chicken stock

1 cup sake (or vodka)

1 cup mirin (sweetened Chinese rice wine)

½ cup sugar

Makes about 30

Small versions of yakitori, one of the best-known of all Japanese dishes, can be made for a party. Chicken thighs have better flavor and are always used in this dish.

To make the sauce, put all the sauce ingredients in a saucepan, bring to a boil and simmer for 15 minutes—the quantity should be reduced by about one-third. Remove from the heat, let cool, then chill until ready to use (no more than 2 days). Pour half the mixture into a small dipping bowl and reserve the remainder.

Thread the chicken and vegetables onto the skewers. For a meal, 5 pieces would be threaded onto each skewer. For fingerfood, use 1 piece each of chicken, scallion or leek, mushroom, and pepper. Leave a little space between each item on the skewer so they will cook through.

Cook under a very hot broiler, turning frequently, until the juices rise to the surface, then paint with the reserved yakitori sauce and continue cooking, turning, and basting until the chicken is done, about 5–10 minutes in all.

Paint once more with the yakitori sauce and serve the skewers on a platter, sprinkled with Japanese 7-spice or black pepper and with the bowl of dipping sauce beside.

Note I also like yakitori with furikake seasoning—a mixture of toasted sesame seeds, red shiso, and nori seaweed, sold in Japanese shops and larger supermarkets.

singapore pork satays

The Chinese food in Singapore is an interesting mixture of traditional Chinese and Southeast Asian influences. Serve these satays with a Chinese-style soy sauce dip, or a Southeast Asian sauce made with fish sauce or peanuts.

Cut the pork into 1-inch slices, then each slice into 1-inch cubes.

Put the coriander seeds in a dry skillet and heat over moderate heat until aromatic. Using a mortar and pestle or spice grinder (or clean coffee mill), grind to a powder. Transfer to a shallow bowl, then add the turmeric, salt, and sugar.

Put the finely sliced lemongrass and shallots in a spice grinder or small blender and work to a paste (add a little water if necessary). Add to the bowl and stir well. Stir in 2 tablespoons of the oil.

Add the cubes of meat and turn to coat in the mixture. Cover and set aside to marinate in the refrigerator for 2 hours or overnight.

Thread 2 pieces of pork onto each soaked skewer and brush with oil. Cook over medium heat on an outdoor grill or under a broiler until done. Thread a piece of cucumber onto the end of each skewer and serve with the sauce.

2 lb. boneless pork loin

1 tablespoon coriander seeds

½ teaspoon ground turmeric

1 teaspoon sea salt

1 tablespoon brown sugar

1 stalk lemongrass, finely sliced

5 small shallots, finely chopped

½ cup sunflower or peanut oil

1 cucumber, quartered lengthwise, seeded, and sliced crosswise

1 quantity dipping sauce, such as soy sauce, Satay Sauce (opposite), or Nuòc Cham (page 119), to serve

20 bamboo skewers, soaked in water for at least 30 minutes

Makes 20

indonesian beef satays

Satay sauce, made with peanuts, is one of Indonesia's best-known contributions to world cuisine. Make these skewers with other meats, such as chicken or pork—even lamb—and serve with the creamy, spicy sauce.

1 lb. lean beef

½ cup coconut milk

juice of 2 limes (about ⅓ cup)

2 fresh red chiles, finely chopped

3 stalks lemongrass, finely chopped

3 garlic cloves, minced

2 teaspoons ground coriander

1 teaspoon ground cumin

1 teaspoon ground cardamom

2 tablespoons fish sauce or soy sauce

grated kaffir lime zest

1 teaspoon sugar

peanut oil, for brushing

Satay Sauce, to serve (right)

10 bamboo skewers, soaked in water for at least 30 minutes

Makes about 10

Cut the beef crosswise into thin strips, 2 x ⅛ inch. Mix the coconut milk, lime juice, chile, lemongrass, garlic, cumin, coriander, cardamom, fish sauce or soy sauce, lime zest, and sugar in a bowl. Add the beef strips and stir to coat. Cover and chill for 2 hours or overnight to develop the flavors.

Drain the beef, discarding the marinade. Thread the beef in a zig-zag pattern onto the soaked skewers and cook under a hot broiler or in a skillet (brushed with a film of peanut oil) until browned and tender. Serve on a platter with a small bowl of Satay Sauce.

Satay Sauce Put ½ cup raw peanuts in a dry skillet and toast until light brown. Crush coarsely. Soak 5 dried chiles in boiling water to cover for 30 minutes. Transfer to a blender, add 8 small shallots or 1 onion, 1 crushed garlic clove, 8 almonds, and 1 chopped stalk of lemongrass and work to a paste.

Heat 2 tablespoons peanut oil in a pan, add the chilli mixture, and stir-fry gently for 5 minutes. Add 1 cup coconut milk and simmer, stirring constantly (keep stirring, and don't cover the pan, or the coconut milk will separate). Add 2 teaspoons lime juice, 1 teaspoon brown sugar, a pinch of salt, and the peanuts. Simmer for 2 minutes, let cool a little and serve.

sweet things and drinks

Serving sweet things will help bring your party to a delicious end—and a party's not a party without lots of wonderful drinks. Preferably champagne, of course, but a truly amazing cocktail can't be beaten.

flavored gelato

Serve gelato in spoons or tiny shot glasses (before the advent of wafer cones, ice cream was served in tiny cone-like glasses).

2 cups milk

2 vanilla beans, split lengthwise or ¼ teaspoon best-quality vanilla extract (optional)

3–4 egg yolks

¾ cup sugar

1 cup heavy cream

Your choice of flavorings such as

¼ cup Strega or Grand Marnier

1 lb. ripe peaches poached in ¾ cup sugar, plus water to cover, then peeled, pitted, and puréed

1 basket raspberries or blackberries, either puréed and strained, or crushed with a fork

pulp and seeds of 6 passionfruit

1 cup canned mango purée (Indian is best)

6 pieces of stem ginger, finely chopped, and 6 tablespoons syrup from the jar

Makes about 6–8 cups

To make the basic gelato, heat the milk with the vanilla beans or vanilla extract, until just below boiling point. Set aside to infuse for 15 minutes. Remove the vanilla beans, if using, and scrape out the seeds with the point of a knife. Stir the seeds back into the milk and discard the beans.

Beat the egg yolks until creamy, then beat 2 tablespoons of the hot milk into the egg yolks, then the remaining milk, a little at a time. Add the sugar and stir until dissolved.

Transfer to a double boiler and cook, stirring, over gentle heat until the mixture coats the back of a spoon. Alternatively, put in a bowl set over a pan of simmering water (the water must not touch the bowl), and cook in the same way. Do not let boil, or the mixture will curdle.

Remove from the heat, dip the pan into cold water to stop the cooking process, then cool and stir in the cream. Divide the gelato mixture into 2–4 parts, add a different flavoring to each portion, then churn each one separately in an ice cream making machine.

Transfer to freezer-proof boxes, cover and keep in the freezer until ready to serve. Soften in the refrigerator for about 20 minutes before serving.

mini croissants with mincemeat and brandy cream

Mini croissants are now widely available in supermarkets, especially at Christmas, while croissant dough is available in larger supermarkets year-round. You can stuff these with mincemeat in advance, so all you have to do is reheat them and top with brandy cream just before serving.

24 mini croissants, cheese or plain

1 jar (about 1 lb.) luxury mincemeat

Brandy cream

1 cup heavy cream

3 tablespoons confectioners' sugar

3 tablespoons brandy or Cognac

Serves 24

To make the Brandy Cream, whip the cream and sugar together, then whip in the brandy or Cognac.

Cut a lengthwise slit in the top of each croissant. Press a teaspoon of mincemeat into the slit. (The dish can be prepared ahead to this point.)

Reheat in a preheated oven at 350°F for 5 minutes. Arrange on a serving platter and top each one with a teaspoon of whipped brandy cream.

Note If mini croissants aren't available, you can make your own using the canned ready-to-bake kind—8 oz. makes 6. You open the can and the dough emerges, ready-cut into 6 triangles for you to roll up and bake yourself. Cut each triangle into 4 smaller triangles (cut off the point, then cut the remaining piece into 3), giving 24 small triangles. Roll up from the long edge leaving the point on top. Bake according to the package instructions, usually at 400°F, but for a shorter time, about 10 minutes, until puffed and golden brown.

mini christmas cakes

At Christmas, everyone will have had their fill of Christmas cake. But it's always nice to suggest the season.

1 section of moist Christmas cake, about 8 x 3 x 3 inches deep

1 package fondant icing, about 1 lb.

Makes about 70 pieces

Cut the sides, top and base off the Christmas cake with a very sharp knife, giving smooth edges. Cut the cake into 1-inch strips lengthwise. Cut each strip into 1-inch strips to make square logs.

Roll out the fondant icing to about ⅛-inch thick, then, using a sharp knife and a metal ruler, cut out rectangular strips 8 x 5 inches wide.

Place one cake "log" on one of the strips and wrap the fondant around it. Press to seal, tap each surface onto the work surface to form sharp corners. Cover with plastic and chill in the refrigerator for at least 30 minutes.

Just before serving, cut the "logs" into 1-inch lengths and serve, perhaps with strong espresso coffee.

mango and ginger kir royale

Kir Royale is cassis with champagne. For my mango and ginger version, I use canned Indian Alphonso mango purée when I'm outside mango growing country. You can also use frozen mango, blended while still frozen to an icy purée. If using fresh or frozen mangoes, you'll have to add a little lemon juice to develop the flavor, plus ice to help smash the fiber.

1 jar stem ginger, pieces cut into quarters

2 cups mango purée

¼ cup ginger purée or juice

syrup from the jar of stem ginger

sugar (to taste)

6 bottles chilled champagne (8 glasses per bottle for champagne cocktails)

Makes at least 50 glasses

Thread the quarter pieces of ginger lengthwise onto a long toothpick or bamboo skewer. Arrange them on a plate, ginger ends downward.

Working in batches if necessary, put the mango purée in a blender, add the ginger purée or juice, the syrup from the jar, and 1 cup ice water and blend well.

Add sugar to taste. Blend again, then add more ice water until the mixture is the texture of thin cream. (If it's too thick it falls to the bottom of the glass.)

Arrange champagne flutes on serving trays, then put 1 teaspoon of the mango mixture in each one. Add a small teaspoon of champagne, stir and set aside until your guests arrive. When they do, top up the glasses with champagne (twice, because they bubble like mad), then put a ginger toothpick across the top of each one and tell your guests it's a swizzle stick.

Everyone will want more, so have extra mango mixture at hand.

mint mojito

½ cup white rum

juice of 2 limes

2 tablespoons sugar or sugar syrup

leaves from a large bunch of mint

ice cubes

sparkling mineral water (optional)

mint sprigs and lime zest, to serve

Serves 2

Caribbean Mojitos are the coolest of all rum drinks. Before serving, pour through a fine-mesh strainer to remove all the chopped mint (it's the mint juice that gives it color).

Put the rum, lime juice, sugar or sugar syrup, mint leaves, and ice cubes in a blender, blend well, then strain into glasses half-filled with ice.

Serve straight or topped up with sparkling mineral water, with a sprig of mint and a curl of lime zest.

frozen margarita

⅓ cup freshly squeezed lime juice, plus extra for the glass

sea salt, for the glass

⅓ cup Triple Sec or Cointreau

½ cup tequila

crushed ice

1 lime, halved and finely sliced lengthwise, to serve

Serves 6

Margaritas are everybody's favorites. Dipping the glass in salt is optional, but the slice of lime definitely isn't.

Upturn the rim of each glass in a saucer of lime juice, then in a second saucer of salt.

Put the lime juice, Triple Sec, and tequila in a blender with crushed ice. Blend until frothy. The sound of the motor will suddenly change as the froth rises above the blades.

Pour into the chilled, salt-rimmed Margarita glasses and serve with a slice of lime.

strawberry margarita

The ultimate girly drink!

1 basket ripe strawberries (about 12)

1 cup tequila

1 tablespoon powdered sugar or superfine sugar

juice of 1 lime

1 tablespoon strawberry syrup

crushed ice

Serves 6

Put all the ingredients in a blender with crushed ice. Blend and serve as in the previous recipe.

swedish glögg

2 bottles dry red wine (750 ml each)

1 bottle aquavit or vodka (750 ml)

12 cardamom pods, crushed

8 whole cloves

1 orange

1 inch fresh ginger, sliced

1 cinnamon stick

1⅔ cups sugar, or to taste

1⅓ cups blanched almonds

1¼ cups raisins

cinnamon sticks, for stirring (optional)

Serves about 20

Glögg is the Scandinavian version of glühwein or mulled wine—I much prefer it.

Using a vegetable peeler or canelle knife, remove the peel from the orange in a single curl (do not include any of the bitter white pith).

Put everything except the almonds and the cinnamon sticks in a bowl or non-reactive saucepan and set aside overnight (at least 12 hours).

Just before serving, heat to just below boiling point, then remove from the heat and stir in the almonds. Do not let boil or the alcohol will be burned off.

Serve in glass punch cups or tea glasses, with little spoons so people can scoop out the almonds and raisins. Small cinnamon sticks make delicious, scented stirrers.

Note If you prefer, omit the almonds and strain out the raisins before serving.

dry martini

This is the finest and best of all cocktails, the dryest dry martini. Traditionally served with an olive, I prefer it "Up with a Twist" (no rocks, with a twist of lemon). Many people prefer martinis made with vodka, so offer an alternative if you like. The classic mixture, by the way, isn't as dry as this—it's one part dry vermouth to three parts gin.

1 measure best-quality gin

1–2 drops of dry vermouth

a curl of lemon zest or an olive on a toothpick

Serves 1

Stir the gin and vermouth together with ice, then strain into martini glasses.

pimm's

This traditional English summertime drink is perfect for parties. When borage is in flower, freeze the pretty blue blossoms in ice cubes for out-of-season Pimm's drinks. Allow 1 cup per drink, and at least 2 drinks per person—but be prepared for repeat orders!

1 part Pimm's

3 parts gingerale, lemonade, or soda

borage flowers

curls of cucumber peel

sliced lemons

sprigs of mint

Serves 1 or a party

Put all ingredients into a pitcher of ice, stir, and serve.

blue champagne

Spectacularly cool, this is one you should only serve if you want your guests merry in seconds. Serve to the firstcomers—otherwise everyone will want one!

2 teaspoons freshly squeezed lemon juice

½ teaspoon Triple Sec

½ teaspoon blue curaçao

½ cup vodka

champagne or other sparkling wine

Serves 2

Put ice cubes in a cocktail shaker, then add the lemon juice, Triple Sec, curaçao, and vodka.

Shake, then strain into 2 champagne flutes and top up with champagne.

Note Triple Sec is best, but can be difficult to find. Use any dry orange-flavored liqueur instead—Cointreau is the most common.

kir cocktails

There are other delicious cocktails, all variations on popular kir.

1 teaspoon of a liqueur such as Poire William, peach or strawberry liqueur, framboise, Midori, or Galliano and the pulp of 1 passionfruit

alternatively, ¼ cup fruit juice, such as pear, pineapple, peach, or apricot

champagne or other sparkling wine

Serves 1

Put 1 teaspoon of liqueur or ¼ cup fruit juice in a champagne flute or coupé and top with champagne.

Note The glass is sometimes decorated with a slice of the fruit concerned.

cranberry cooler

Cranberry mixed with citrus juice is a marriage made in heaven—the prettiest, cloudy pink. It's great with vodka in a Sea Breeze, but this soft version is irresistible too.

4 cups cranberry juice

4 cups orange juice

ice cubes

sparkling mineral water

twists of orange peel, to serve

Serves 20

Mix the cranberry and orange juices in a pitcher.

Put the ice in tall glasses, half-fill with the cranberry mixture and stir well. Top with sparkling mineral water and serve with a twist of orange peel.

soft tropical sangria

A non-alcoholic version of the traditional wine-based sangria, but with a South American twist. Use any fruit, but include tropicals, like mango, pineapple, or starfruit. Don't use any that go "furry," such as melon, kiwifruit, or strawberries. Wonderful for a summer party in the garden.

1 ripe mango, finely sliced

1 lime, finely sliced

1 lemon, finely sliced

½ pineapple, cut lengthwise into 6–8 wedges, then finely sliced to form triangles

1 starfruit (carambola), sliced

3 tablespoons sugar

8 cups gingerale or lemonade, well chilled

Serves about 12

Put the sliced fruit in a punch bowl. Sprinkle with sugar and set aside for at least 30 minutes. Top with icy gingerale or lemonade just before serving. Fill wine glasses with ice, add a few pieces of the fruit, then top with the fizzy liquid.

Variation Peachy Sangria

Put 2 cups peach nectar, mint sprigs, and 2 sliced peaches in the bowl and top with gingerale or lemonade (or champagne).

index

conversion chart

Weights and measures have been
rounded up or down slightly to make
measuring easier.

Volume equivalents:

American	Metric	Imperial
1 teaspoon	5 ml	
1 tablespoon	15 ml	
¼ cup	60 ml	2 fl.oz.
⅓ cup	75 ml	2½ fl.oz.
½ cup	125 ml	4 fl.oz.
⅔ cup	150 ml	5 fl.oz. (¼ pint)
¾ cup	175 ml	6 fl.oz.
1 cup	250 ml	8 fl.oz.

Weight equivalents:

Imperial	Metric
1 oz.	25 g
2 oz.	50 g
3 oz.	75 g
4 oz.	125 g
5 oz.	150 g
6 oz.	175 g
7 oz.	200 g
8 oz. (½ lb.)	250 g
9 oz.	275 g
10 oz.	300 g
11 oz.	325 g
12 oz.	375 g
13 oz.	400 g
14 oz.	425 g
15 oz.	475 g
16 oz. (1 lb.)	500 g
2 lb.	1 kg

Measurements:

Inches	Cm
¼ inch	5 mm
½ inch	1 cm
¾ inch	1.5 cm
1 inch	2.5 cm
2 inches	5 cm
3 inches	7 cm
4 inches	10 cm
5 inches	12 cm
6 inches	15 cm
7 inches	18 cm
8 inches	20 cm
9 inches	23 cm
10 inches	25 cm
11 inches	28 cm
12 inches	30 cm

Oven temperatures:

110°C	(225°F)	Gas ¼
120°C	(250°F)	Gas ½
140°C	(275°F)	Gas 1
150°C	(300°F)	Gas 2
160°C	(325°F)	Gas 3
180°C	(350°F)	Gas 4
190°C	(375°F)	Gas 5
200°C	(400°F)	Gas 6
220°C	(425°F)	Gas 7
230°C	(450°F)	Gas 8
240°C	(475°F)	Gas 9